Scottish Sea Kayaking

FIFTY GREAT SEA KAYAK VOYAGES

Doug Cooper & George Reid

PESDA PRESS

WWW.PESDAPRESS.COM

First published in Great Britain 2005 by Pesda Press
Reprinted with minor updates 2008

Pesda Press
Galeri22
Doc Victoria
Caernarfon
Gwynedd
LL55 1SQ
UK

Distributed by Cordee
3a DeMontfort Street
Leicester
LE1 7HD
UK

Printed in Poland, produced by Polskabook .

Introduction

Scotland has some of the most varied and dramatic coastline in the world. This includes fast tidal streams and calm sea lochs, huge cliffs and sandy beaches, history and culture and an abundance of wildlife. The weather and oceans have been shaping this environment for millions of years and nowadays it offers the last true wilderness of Great Britain. The coastline provides an archipelago of islands guarding the Atlantic coast to the west, remote and dominant cliffs towering above the tidal streams of the north and sea stacks, arches and wildlife fronting the North Sea to the east. The Scottish coastline offers a lifetime of exploration for everyone.

This guide is born from a love of this coastal wilderness, and a desire to discover and explore it. The sea kayak is the perfect craft to journey through this amazing environment at close quarters, and in this gives a unique perspective on the surroundings. The authors have paddled the entire Scottish coastline and have had many years of pleasure in discovering the variety it offers. It is from this experience that fifty sea kayaking trips have been chosen.

The fifty trips described are not necessarily the 'best', but are intended to give a real insight into the variety of kayaking the Scottish coastline offers. The authors are aware that many fantastic areas have been missed out, notably Orkney and Shetland. Our descriptions are not full in each trip and the weather as we know makes the same trip different each time; this should allow the paddler to still have the opportunity to discover things while paddling our trips. In addition to this it is hoped that the trips will provide something for all abilities of sea kayaker, with the trips ranging from sheltered lochs to committing tidal races. The guide is designed to provide all the relevant tidal information and route descriptions to enable the kayaker to head off and enjoy the trip. The kayaker will still need to have the knowledge to interpret this information and use it wisely in the sea environment, taking into account the appropriate safety considerations. The guide is about more than this though; it also provides an insight into the history, culture and wildlife that makes the Scottish coastline that extra bit special. Resulting from years of kayaking, research and personal experiences this guide will provide the true flavour of what makes up Scottish sea kayaking.

Contents

Contents

Important Notice

As with many outdoor activities that take place in remote and potentially hostile environments, technical ability, understanding of the environment and good planning are essential. The sea is one of the most committing environments of all, and with this considered it should be treated with the constant respect that it deserves. This guide is designed to provide information that will inspire the sea kayaker to venture into this amazing environment, however it cannot provide the essential ingredients of ability, environmental awareness and good planning. Before venturing out on any of the trips described in this book ensure that your knowledge and ability are appropriate to the seriousness of the trip. If you are unsure, then look for appropriate advice before embarking on the trips described. The book is purely a guide to provide information about the sea kayaking trips. For the additional essential knowledge of safety at sea, personal paddling, environmental considerations and tidal planning the authors recommend gaining the appropriate training from experienced and qualified individuals.

Warning

Sea kayaking is inherently a potentially dangerous sport, and with this considered, users of this guide should take the appropriate precautions before undertaking any of the trips. The information supplied in this book has been well researched, however the authors can take no responsibility if tidal times differ or information supplied is not sufficient. Conditions can change quickly and dramatically on the sea and there is no substitute for personal experience and judgment when kayaking or during the planning stages of a sea trip.

The guide is no substitute for personal ability, personal risk assessment and good judgement. The decision on whether to go out sea kayaking or not, and any consequences arising from that decision, remain yours and yours alone.

Photographs

All photos by Doug Cooper and George Reid.

About the Authors

Doug Cooper

Doug has spent his entire life involved with the outdoors. At age seven he was introduced to scrambling amongst the Lakeland mountains, and first sat in a kayak at thirteen. Since these early days it has become Doug's career as well as his first love on a day off. Through work and play it has led to expeditions and trips to many of the remoter corners of the world. At present Doug is based at Scotland's National Outdoor Training Centre, Glenmore Lodge. Here Doug is Head of Paddlesports working as a Level 5 Sea and Inland Coach, as well as a Mountain Instructor. It is in this work that he realises his real passion, which is coaching and introducing people to an activity and an environment that has given him so much over the years. Doug has been exploring the Scottish coastline in a sea kayak since 1990 and in this time has grown to love this amazing natural environment. Through work and play he has also sea kayaked many other fantastic areas of the United Kingdom. In addition to this he has enjoyed expeditions to Greenland, Norway and Iceland using the sea kayak to explore the coastlines and cultures. As long as he is in the outdoors coaching, exploring and learning, then there is nowhere else he would rather be.

George Reid

George is known to many outdoor folk through his work with Glenmore Lodge (Scotland's National Outdoor Training Centre) that has spanned a period of 20 years. He became an International Mountain Guide (IFMGA) in 1987, subsequently working in the European Alps and the Canadian Rockies guiding rock and ice climbs, making ascents of Alpine peaks and leading ski mountaineering trips. Despite being introduced to sea and river kayaking at school in Edinburgh during the mid 80's, George focused his attentions on mountaineering. It was not until 1996, when at Glenmore Lodge, that George was exposed to the scope of sea kayaking.

It was his wife Catriona who suggested that George should "join the dots". She bought him a map of Scotland, pencilled in the trips done, and that in turn focussed the weekends and holidays for the next few years until a continuous line appeared on the map around the mainland of Scotland. If there is one thread that links all George's adventures it is an appreciation of nature. His knowledge of the flora and fauna, be it on the mountain or the sea, is well known and one of the greatest pleasures he receives is when he can share these experiences with other people.

How to Use the Guide

To use the guide all that you will need are up-to-date tide timetables of the relevant area, the appropriate Ordnance Survey map and the knowledge to use these. There is also a Trip Planning Route Card at the end of the book that can be used to help plan your chosen trip. There is a full explanation of how to use this alongside the route card. Each of the fifty trip chapters is set out into six sections:

Tidal & Route Information - This is designed as a quick reference for all the 'must know' information on which to plan the trip yourself.

Introduction - This is designed to give the reader a brief overview of what to expect from the trip and whet the appetite.

Description - This provides further detail on the trip including coastline information, launching/landing information, about the wildlife and environment, historical information and the views to expect.

Tide & Weather - Giving further tidal information and how best to plan the trip, taking the tides, weather and local knowledge into consideration.

Map of Route - An outline of the route's start/finish points, landing places, points of interest and tidal information.

Additional Information - Further information that will help complete the trip, or is of interest if in the area.

Using the Tidal & Route Information

Trip name

Trip number

Grade - (Colour scheme indicated)

 A- Single day trips from 6 – 20 kilometres in distance. Relatively easy landings with escape routes available. Offering relative shelter from extreme conditions and little affected by ocean swell. Some tidal movement may be found, but easy to predict with no tidal races or overfalls.

 B - Mainly day trips from 10 – 30 kilometres in distance. Some awkward landings and sections of coastline with no escape routes should be expected. Tidal movement, tidal races, overfalls, crossings, ocean swell and surf may be found on these trips. They will also be exposed to the weather and associated conditions.

 C- Single and multi-day trips from 25 – 93 kilometres in distance. These trips will have difficult landings and will have no escape routes for the majority of the trip. Fast tidal movement, tidal races, overfalls, extended crossings, ocean swell and surf will be found on all these trips. They will be very exposed to the weather and conditions, therefore requiring detailed planning. With this considered they will all require good conditions for the trip to be viable.

Distance - Total distance for trip or for each day on multi-day trips.

Average time - Worked out on 5km/h including stops and some exploration where appropriate.

OS Sheet - Number of Ordnance Survey 1:50,000 Landranger map required.

Tidal Port - The port for which tide timetables will be required to work out the tidal streams.

Start - Symbol used on map, name and six-figure grid reference of starting point.

Finish - Symbol used on map, name and six-figure grid reference of finishing point.

HW/LW - The tidal time difference from the tidal port of high water and low water for the local port nearest to the trip.

Tidal times - The position of the tidal stream movement: followed by the direction to which the tidal stream flows and the time it starts flowing in relation to the tidal port high water.

Tidal rates - The areas in which the tidal streams are fastest and the speed in knots of the average spring rate.

Coastguard - Name of the relevant Coastguard Station. The telephone number and the time the three-hourly weather forecast starts. Being announced on the VHF radio on Channel 16.

Below is an example:

Point of Stoer

No. 26 | Grade B | 17km | 5 Hours | OS Sheet 15 | Tidal Port Ullapool

Start	△ Clashnessie (058309)
Finish	◎ Stoer (038283)
HW/LW	HW/LW at Lochinver is around 5 minutes before Ullapool.
Tidal times	Off the Point of Stoer: SW stream starts about 5 hrs 10 mins after HW Ullapool. NE stream starts about 2 hrs 15 mins before HW Ullapool.
Tidal rates	The average spring rate here can reach 2.5 knots off the Point of Stoer.
Coastguard	Stornoway, tel: 01851 702013, VHF Weather 0710 UT

Map Symbols Used

 - Start

 - Finish

- Described Route

○ - Landing Place

 - Lighthouse

 - Beacon

■ - Castle

▪ - Building or Built-up Area

⌃ - Possible Rough Water

 - Tidal Stream Direction

+0550 Ullapool - Time in relation to High Water of Tidal Port

2.5 Kn Sp - Average Spring Rate

Scottish Outdoor Access Code

Access to the outdoors in Scotland is encouraged; visitors and locals have a right of responsible access. Scottish Natural Heritage (SNH) is responsible for promoting and publicising the Scottish Outdoor Access Code (SOAC).

Where you have access rights to is not shown on Ordnance Survey maps, or any other map in Scotland. The Scottish Outdoor Access Code deals with the land and freshwater access which is pertinent to the sea kayaker as you have to gain access to the sea over land or down a river and then again land to camp, walk or rest.

You are completely free to kayak on the sea; there is no limit how far offshore you can travel. However, for safety rather than access reasons, the further you travel offshore, during a crossing to an island for example, the more reason there is to contact the Coastguard and let them know your plans.

The Scottish Outdoor Access Code is based on three key principles and these apply equally to the public and to land managers.

Respect the interests of other people

Acting with courtesy, consideration and awareness is very important. If you are exercising access rights, make sure that you respect the privacy, safety and livelihoods of those living or working in the outdoors, and the needs of other people enjoying the outdoors. If you are a land manager, respect people's use of the outdoors and their need for a safe and enjoyable visit.

Care for the environment

If you are exercising access rights, look after the places you visit and enjoy, and leave the land as you find it. If you are a land manager, help maintain the natural and cultural features which make the outdoors attractive to visit and enjoy.

Take responsibility for your own actions

If you are exercising access rights, remember that the outdoors cannot be made risk-free and act with care at all times for your own safety and that of others. If you are a land manager, act with care at all times for people's safety.

Getting more advice and information

The Scottish Outdoor Access Code cannot cover every possible situation, setting or activity. Free information and advice on access rights and responsibilities, and on who to contact in your local authority is available online at www.outdooraccess-scotland.com.

Mull of Galloway

No. 1 | Grade C | 25km | 6 Hours | OS Sheet 82 | Tidal Port Greenock & Liverpool

Start	△ Drummore (135367)
Finish	◎ Port Logan (094404)
HW/LW	HW/LW at Drummore is about 30 mins after Liverpool.
Tidal times	From the Mull of Galloway up to Port Logan: The NW then N stream start about 2 hrs and 50 mins before HW Greenock. The S then SE stream starts about 3 hrs and 10 mins after HW Greenock.
	At a point about 3km SSE of the Mull of Galloway: The WSW stream starts about 1 hr after HW Liverpool. The E going stream starts about 5 hrs before HW Liverpool.
Tidal rates	The average spring rate along the west coast is 5 knots.
	At a point about 3km SSE from the Mull of Galloway the average spring rate is 4 knots.
	On the east side of the peninsula, there is a bay between Cailiness Point (153356) and the Mull of Galloway. There is an eddy which runs north to south in this bay when the main stream is flowing eastward past the Mull of Galloway.
Coastguard	Clyde, tel:01475 729988, VHF weather 0820 UT Liverpool, tel:0151 9313341, VHF weather 0730 UT

Mull of Galloway foghorn

Introduction

This is a lively place to visit especially early in the summer when many seabirds are in residence, nesting on the cliffs. Many thousands of birds, a mixture of guillemots, razorbills and puffins use the cliffs to rear their young between the months of April and July.

Not only is the air busy with birds, but also the cliffs, and where the cliffs are not so steep they are often lined with anglers hoping to catch 'a big one'.

As for the sea, it is notably active as well. Being a significant promontory, the Mull of Galloway would always be a place to look out for a strong tidal stream, but add to this the fact that this marks the southern entrance to the North Channel, the narrow lane of water that separates Northern Ireland from Scotland and you have the makings of an even livelier piece of water.

Description

The east side of the Mull of Galloway is a tame place in comparison to the west side, so starting at Drummore provides a gentle introduction. Within a short time after starting you will round Cailiness Point, here you might notice the effects of the eddy that circulates in the bay to your south. Far out to your left, about 11km distant are the 'Scares'; who they first scared and when can only be imagined. The Scares are a breeding site for around 2000 pairs of gannets.

If you have decided to do this trip when the wind is coming from the NE, stopping at East Tarbet might be awkward, but it does at least have a sandy landing at periods of lower water. Your timing for arriving at the most easterly point, Lagvag (159306), will be crucial so you round this point hopefully into the shelter when the tidal streams are not active.

Rounding the Mull, watch out for fishing lines, especially in the height of the summer holidays; if it is a fine day there is a good chance that anglers will be dotted around all over the rocks. This is a very beautiful section of the coast. The rocks are covered in a lovely striking yellow lichen and there are many birds nesting on the cliffs in the springtime. There are one or two caves here, one with fine lime-flows that would eventually build up into stalactites if it wasn't for the pounding of the sea.

Take the opportunity to have a break at West Tarbet, though only a narrow channel has been cleared of rocks, as the next stopping point is likely to be 7km further on at Portencorkrie, depending on the sea state. The tidal stream should be noticeable on your journey north now, a fine helping hand to whisk you up toward Port Logan.

A race forms off Crammag Head, extending for up to 2 miles to the south. It is unlikely that you will be venturing out into the heart of this race, but even close in at this head and other bits of the coast expect there to be noticeable activity.

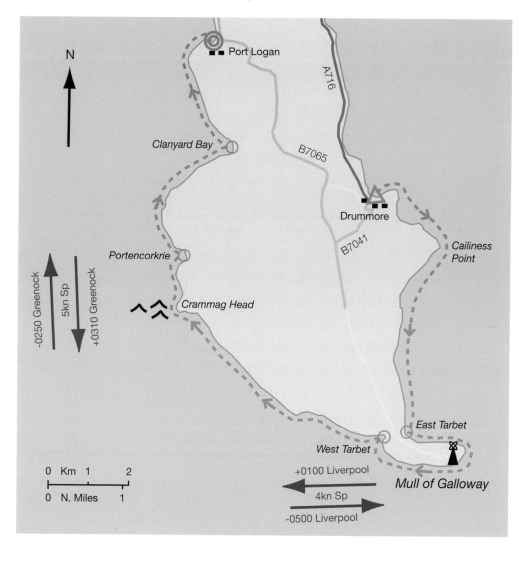

Port Logan at the end of the trip is a quiet little harbour that recently hit the limelight when it was chosen as the location to film '2000 Acres of Sky'. This far south harbour was 'faking' it as a harbour on an island off the west coast of Scotland, where the scene for the story was set. Prior to this recent claim to fame, Port Logan was recognised as one of the first places to farm fish. In the 1800's a tidal pool was excavated and used as a fish larder holding cod, where they would be kept live and fresh until needed for the table. Today you can visit the fishpond as a modern tourist attraction.

Tide & Weather

The tidal streams in this area are very strong, and each headland will produce noticeable turbulence. Expect to come across eddies on the journey north to Port Logan. The most efficient way to kayak this trip is to arrive at the Mull of Galloway (Lagvag) -0200 HW Liverpool, you might have a bit of tide to work against at the Mull, but later on in the trip you should reap the benefits of this early start.

If you allow enough time you could land at East Tarbet and then walk up to the lighthouse and view the sea state and tidal stream speed prior to continuing your journey, thereby accommodating any difference in the printed time of the change in direction of the tidal streams.

Additional Information

Luce Bay is noted on the map as a 'Danger Area'. Contact 'Luce Bay Range' tel: 01 776 888 741 to find out if the range is active or inactive prior to setting out on your proposed journey.

An alternative less committing trip can be done from West Tarbet to East Tarbet or vice versa, if you only have a small window of opportunity.

Ailsa Craig

No. 2 | Grade C | 32km | 7 Hours | OS Sheet 76 | Tidal Port Greenock

Start	△ Lendalfoot - Carleton Bay (123894)
Finish	◎ Lendalfoot - Carleton Bay (123894)
HW/LW	HW/LW at Girvan is about 30 mins before HW/LW Greenock.
Tidal times	The S going stream starts about 15 mins before HW Greenock. The N going stream starts about 6 hrs and 15 mins before HW Greenock.
Tidal rates	The rate of either stream is not very great, reaching 0.6 knots on an average spring tide.
Coastguard	Clyde, tel:01475 729988, VHF Weather 0810 UT

Introduction

A longish crossing over to a very significant landmark, known as Paddy's Milestone, due to the fact that it is close to halfway between Belfast in Northern Ireland and Glasgow in Scotland.

Ailsa Craig has withstood the ravages of time and most notably the effects of glaciation. What you see today is all that remains of a plug of rock that sat deep within an ancient volcano. The

Ailsa Craig lighthouse

volcano eroded away, leaving the hard micro-granite which is famous for being a superb rock to make curling stones from.

The glaciers of the Ice Age removed not only the surrounding volcanic rock, but also some of the micro-granite, allowing geologists to plot the route taken by the flows of ice down as far as Wales.

Ailsa Craig is a long established breeding ground for gannets. The rising numbers of nesting birds, c 34,000 in 1995, means that Ailsa Craig is one of the biggest gannet colonies in the world.

Description

Leaving Carleton Bay you might see one or two common seals in amongst the rocks to your left along with a few shags.

With a calm sea there is a good chance that you will see a porpoise on your journey, but also keep an eye open for basking sharks. There are not so many basking sharks around as there used to be, perhaps a direct result of fishing for them, as was done in these waters by an Ayrshire fisherman Howard McCrindle from the 1970's up to 1993. This was the last of the shark fisheries in Scotland to close, when his boat was decommissioned in 1993.

If you travel out in the springtime you will notice, well before landfall, a vivid blue wash of colour on the hillside behind and above the lighthouse; this is from the huge carpets of bluebells that cover this portion of the island.

Arriving at the island you will quickly realise that there is no easy landing on a sandy beach, rather the opposite, boulders line the shore. If the tide is low there will be weed over the rocks affording a bit of protection for your kayak. It is possible to land to the left of the lighthouse or beside the jetty to the right of the lighthouse.

The jetty is somewhat dilapidated, but clear to see is the narrow gauge tramway that was used to transport all manner of things, but most notably the curling stones that were made from the high quality micro-granite rock taken from further along the north coast. It is well worth the time to walk along the old railway, which hugs the cliff and crosses gullies on its way to the quarry, as it is more difficult to land below the quarry.

Above the lighthouse up on the hill stands an old castle that was originally built at least six centuries ago by monks from Crossraguel Abbey in Ayrshire. As with all the lighthouses, this light is now unmanned. The living quarters have succumbed to the ravages of the weather, with broken windows being the norm. Inside some of the rooms you can see furniture, beds with their linen still on, books and paperwork, as though there wasn't time to clear everything up prior to leaving.

Leaving the jetty and continuing round the island in an anticlockwise direction, you will paddle adjacent to the railway that goes to the quarry. At the end of the quarry there is a large old rusting foghorn.

From here the cliff scenery becomes more spectacular, as does the bird life. Gannets wheel in the air above you, guillemots and razorbills come sweeping down to land on the water.

There is a reef of rocks at the SW corner, in behind which you might find a bit of sheltered water and a chance to land.

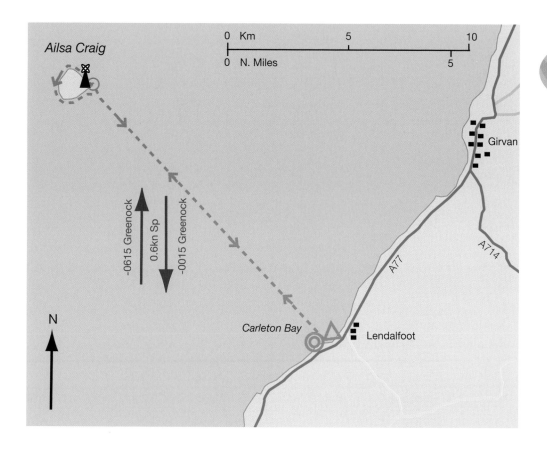

From here returning to the lighthouse, there is a good chance that there will be some of our larger seals, the Atlantic grey seal, hauled out on the rocks.

Tide & Weather

The tidal streams are weak, yet due to the fact that this island obstructs the flow of the sea, expect there to be a little bit more activity around the island close to the shore.

If you have chosen a period with light easterly winds, be aware that the afternoon winds are often stronger than those in the morning, and if they increase as the day goes on, the journey home could be a bit harder than planned.

Additional Information

The Sea-Cat ferry that sails from Troon to Belfast speeds past Ailsa Craig, either on the east or the west of the island. It is worthwhile phoning the operations manager (02890 313103) for Sea-Cat to establish what the sailing times and route will be on the day you plan to cross.

Ailsa Craig is a nature reserve and as such benefits from being disturbed as little as possible; it is best to make this trip a day visit and not to overnight on the island.

In years gone by there were rats on the island, these rodents predated heavily on the bird life. In an attempt to improve the survival rate of the birds, much rat poison has been used on the island. If you find any cereal grains, such as wheat dyed a blue/black colour, do not handle this, as it is very poisonous.

Mull of Kintyre

No. 3 | Grade C | 24km | 5-6 Hours | OS Sheet 68 | Tidal Port Oban

Start	△ Keil Point (670077)
Finish	◎ Uisaed (627207)
HW/LW	HW & LW at Machrihanish varies between 5 hrs and 30 mins and 4 hrs before Oban.
Tidal times	The N going stream starts at about 4 hrs after HW Oban. The S going stream starts at about 2 hrs and 30 mins before HW Oban.
Tidal rates	The north-going and the south-going stream both reach 5 knots on an average spring tide.
Coastguard	Clyde, tel:01475 729988, VHF Weather 0810 UT

Introduction

A peninsula with a reputation!

It's not easy to approach a significant trip like this without a wee bit of apprehension. Tales of turbulence, enough to capsize previous kayakers, others taking the Vikings' route. Why did the Vikings cross from East Loch Tarbert to West Loch Tarbert? To claim the peninsula below

Sanda Island

is the message we get from the historians. What if the great mariners had recognised the Mull of Kintyre was a place to avoid? Perhaps it is too wild a place for a kayak. 20kms of rugged coast without easy landings and 5 knots of flow to help or hinder.

Description

A small car park gives easy access to the shore. The view from Carskey Bay does not allow for a preview of what is to come, yet it is not without interest. Looking over the sand into the crystal clear water where gannets dive may remind you of trips to the remoter parts of the NW of Scotland.

Within 2km of starting there is a smaller sandy beach (653072). Seriously consider stopping here for a quick break, quite similar to driving in the remoter parts of Scotland, where the signs say 'last petrol for 50 miles'; this is the last easy comfort stop until close to the end of the trip.

At Sron Uamha, a little sticky out bit, Sron is 'nose or promontory' in Gaelic, the first of the tidal races will be met. So from here on round, expect a bit of action at each of the 'sticky out bits of land'.

The Gaelic name for Mull of Kintyre is 'ceann-tire', meaning 'lands end'. It must have been named on a misty day, as Northern Ireland is only c.20km away. It was from Antrim, the county only 20km away, that the Scots came to settle in what we now know as Scotland more than 1500 years ago.

A small white building, up on the cliff at Rubha na Lice, has below it a sea stack. No ordinary sea stack, but one with a graceful curving 'S' shaped crack in it. Climbers don't rush! It looks awfully like an off-width, so unless you are a champion arm barring jammer, keep paddling!

Very soon you pass 'South Point', but it is on the west coast, named by a Scot obviously.

The lighthouse just looks normal, white and deserted, unless an enthusiastic walker has descended the 300m from the car park. More interesting than the light is the rock architecture, 'red squirrels tufts'. If you live where the grey squirrels have ousted our native reds, be sure to have a look at a picture of a red squirrel and you will see what I mean when you paddle round 'ceann-tire'.

A lot of the rock round here is mica schist, nothing unusual for Scotland, but the way the huge blocks lie at the foot of the very steep hillside is striking. The colourful mixture of grey and green, the obvious parallel bedding planes in the huge blocks, all randomly stacked on top of each other, catch the eye.

A large sweeping cliff, coloured by bands of lovely cream-coloured rock, descends from Dun Ban to Rubha Duin Bhain.

Uamh Ropa is true to its name, one sea cave and two dry caves above the present sea level that would give animals shelter. Looking at the OS map, and at the ground as you pass by, it is easy to assume that no one would be able to visit the caves, other than from the sea, but people can make their way down the hillside, no doubt following the tracks of sheep that have negotiated the steep ground masterfully.

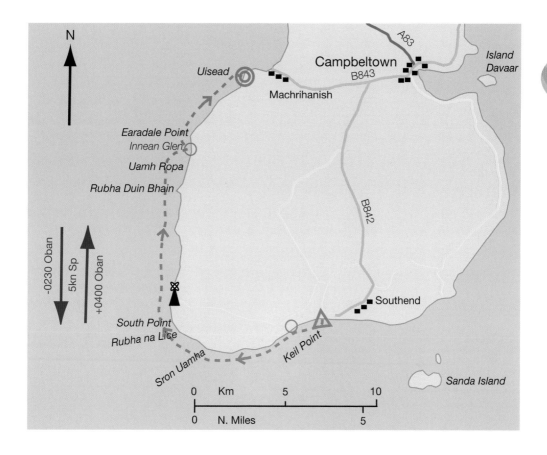

One kilometre further on there is a beach at the foot of Innean Glen. A sandy beach with rocks studded on its chest and more than likely a wee bit of surf. To land or not to land? From the start it is 18km to this point, so a comfort stop might be uppermost in your mind!

An obvious white cross sits back from the shore on the grass at the left side of the well grazed flat area. Not so obvious might be the wild goats, well camouflaged against the hillside.

If you don't fancy trying to land through the 'surf n'studs', it might be possible to sneak in on the left side by a wet exit amongst some sharp rocks with only a bit of swell to contend with. Which is best? Only you will know on the day.

The cross marks 'The Sailor's Grave' as it is known, the inscription on the cross 'God Knows' tells more. The body was unidentifiable; nobody knows where it came from. A grave was dug on May 16th 1917 and surrounded by round white quartz stones.

Shortly after leaving you will round Earadale Point. The journey now takes you NE, the backdrop tames, there will be other landing opportunities almost too late, as the finish is only 4-5km from 'The Sailor's Grave'.

Tide & Weather

Try to get below the lighthouse at the start of the north-going stream (HW Oban plus 4 hours). This is a stretch of 9km, with a possible short break 1.5 km into the trip, so to achieve this consider leaving around 2 hours after HW Oban.

White-beaked dolphin

Dolphins

Scotland is lucky to have 6 different types of dolphin swimming around its coast. Around the bottlenose dolphins in particular a tourist trade has been built; several operators take visitors out in boats to hopefully see the dolphins which on occasion put on superb acrobatic displays. The other dolphins that can be seen are the common, white-sided, white-beaked, striped and risso's dolphin.

Dolphins can at a distance be confused with porpoises, but once closer the smaller size (1.5m) of the porpoise and its lack of beak are helpful identification features, most dolphins are 2.5m in length or greater. For some reason, the dolphins in the Moray Firth on the east coast occasionally play with porpoises in a way not dissimilar to a cat with a mouse, tossing the porpoises into the air repeatedly which unfortunately kills the porpoise.

Remember, most of the little headlands that stick out will more than likely cause the sea to be a bit livelier. If you go with a strong NE or E wind, watch out for the potentially severe downdraughts, and consider what the last 4km will be like, head on into the wind.

If the surfers are 'bumping their gums' due to the lack of surf at Machrihanish, then it's a good day to head out to 'Ceann-tire', and if it happens to be a neap tide, all the better!

Sron Uamha and Sanda Island

Additional Information

The finish is in a little bay just below a cod hatchery, but of more interest is the Machrihanish Seabird Observatory, which stands at the top left of the bay.

Rocky foreshore

Rhinns of Islay

No. 4 | Grade C | 22km | 5 Hours | OS Sheet 60 | Tidal Port Oban

Start	△ Port Charlotte (253583)
Finish	◎ Kilchiaran Bay (200600)
HW/LW	HW/LW at Portnahaven is about 55 minutes before Oban.
Tidal times	Off the Rhinns of Islay:
	The NW going stream starts about 5 hrs and 30 mins after HW Oban. The SE going stream starts about 40 mins before HW Oban.
Tidal rates	There are three areas on this trip where the tidal streams run at their fastest:
	On the south side of the island of Orsay the average spring rate can reach 8 knots.
	On the west side of Frenchman's Rocks the average spring rate can reach 8 knots.
	Between Frenchman's Rocks and Rubha na Faing there is very fast water.
Coastguard	Clyde, tel:01475 729988, VHF Weather 0810 UT

Frenchman's Rocks

Introduction

Islay is perhaps known to most for its malt whisky. Names like Bowmore and Laphroaig will be familiar to those who appreciate a drop of the amber nectar!

The island has a rich history due to it being located so close to Northern Ireland and its fertile land supports the main industries, which are beef cattle and sheep farming. In between visiting all the whisky distilleries there are standing stones, stone circles, chambered cairns and a broch to visit.

For the sea kayaker it has a lot to offer, remote coastlines, interesting wildlife and fast water.

Description

Port Charlotte, with its tidy small whitewashed houses above the shore, on the west side of Loch Indaal is a world apart from the wild west coast of the Rhinns of Islay where you are headed. The small museum in Port Charlotte, illustrating Islay life over the years is well worth visiting. The journey down to Rhinns Point should be straightforward, passing a few fish farms on the way. Up on the land at Nerabus (225551) are a couple of ancient burial grounds, said to house some of the best medieval grave slabs in the whole of Scotland. As you round Rhinns Point, the island of Orsay with its lighthouse built by the famous Stevenson family, will dominate the view. Also on this island there is an ancient chapel.

Prior to arriving at Portnahaven you will probably have spotted a few common seals, which are often to be seen chilling out in the harbour. Fishing used to be the industry that fuelled the economy here, but now many of the houses are holiday homes.

From Portnahaven up to Frenchman's Rocks, depending on your timing, there might be an eddy running along the coast just before you get to Rubha na Faing.

Islay is very rich when it comes to bird life, none of the other Hebrides can surpass it for the number of recorded species, which stands at close to 200. Geese winter on the island in great numbers and the RSPB has designed farming practices that encourage these 20,000 plus visitors to return each year. Islay has the proud distinction of being one of the last strongholds for the very rare chough, a black crow-like bird with red beak and legs.

Around Frenchman's Rocks you are likely to see kittiwakes, but also keep an eye out for skuas, petrels and gannets.

From here northwards the coast is far more rugged, no longer is it closely backed by a road, and the higher cliffs give this section a remote feel to it.

Lossit Bay provides a possible landing and a good chance that you will have this secluded beach to yourself.

Kilchiaran Bay marks the end of this trip, equally it could be the start, you just need to sort out the timings so that you don't arrive at Frenchman's Rocks when it is kicking off.

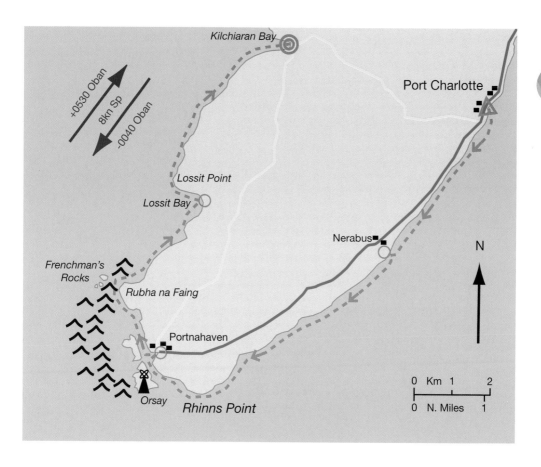

Tide & Weather

The tidal streams in this area are very strong. The planning of your trip will vary greatly depending on what you want to experience.

In Loch Indaal there might be an eddy running down the coast from Port Charlotte to Rhinns Point. If you time your departure so you arrive at Rhinns Point in the last hour of the SE going stream (4 hours 30 minutes after HW Oban) you will then have time to stop at Portnahaven for a break and then set out close to when the NW going stream starts at 5 hours and 30 minutes after HW Oban. This should see you going through the passage between Frenchman's Rocks and Rubha na Faing well before the tide race reaches its maximum.

Those looking for a more exciting and challenging trip might, with due care and additional planning, consider going outside the island of Orsay and also on the outside of Frenchman's Rocks. If there is a swell running, landing on the west coast could be challenging if you are not familiar with surf.

Additional Information

When you drop off the shuttle car at Kilchiaran Bay, be sure to check out the sea state and the size of the surf.

Garbh Eileach

Garvellachs from Arduaine

No. 5 | Grade C | Day 1 - 22km/5hrs | Day 2 - 19km/5hrs | OS Sheet 55 | Tidal Port Oban

Start	△ Arduaine (802099)
Finish	◎ Arduaine (802099)
HW/LW	HW/LW at the Garvellachs is around 10 minutes before Oban.
Tidal times	In Cuan Sound: The SE going stream starts about 2 hrs before HW Oban. The NW going stream starts about 4 hrs and 20 mins after HW Oban.
	Between Garvellachs and Lunga: The SW going stream starts at about 1 hr and 55 mins before HW Oban. The NE going stream starts about 4 hrs and 30 mins after HW Oban.
	In Bealach a Choin Ghlais: The E going stream starts about 2 hrs and 5 mins before HW Oban. The W going stream starts about 4 hrs and 20 mins after HW Oban.
	In Shuna Sound: The N going stream starts about 4 hrs and 30 mins after HW Oban. The S going stream starts about 2 hrs before HW Oban.
Tidal rates	There are five areas on this trip where the tidal streams run at their fastest:

In Cuan Sound the average spring rate can reach 6 knots.
Off Belnahua the average spring rate can reach 6-7 knots.
Between the Garvellachs and Belnahua the average spring rate can reach 2-3 knots.
In Bealach a Choin Ghlais the average spring rate can reach 8.5 knots.
At Shuna Point the average spring rate can reach 1 knot.

Coastguard   Clyde, tel:01475 729988, VHF Weather 0810 UT

Introduction

This is a deservedly popular paddling area in Scotland, and this trip takes in some of the best parts. There is a great blend of history and wildlife on this trip, along with unique geological variety. Throughout the paddle there are strong tidal streams to keep the mind focussed on the navigation. With islands, mountains and sea all around, it is a journey that will be remembered long after it has finished.

Description

Setting off from Arduaine and crossing the mouth of Loch Melfort, you will be paddling through an area sheltered by islands. These islands of Shuna, Luing and Torsa offer some beautiful scenery, which hides the exposure of the journey that lies behind them. Whilst heading to Ardinamir Bay, south of Torsa, there is little tidal movement, something that will change very

soon. Paddling through the scenic narrows between Torsa and Luing the first of the tidal stream will be felt taking you towards Cuan Sound. Watch out for seals and other wildlife whilst being gently helped by this tidal stream. Passing through Cuan Sound you'll paddle round Cuan Point

5

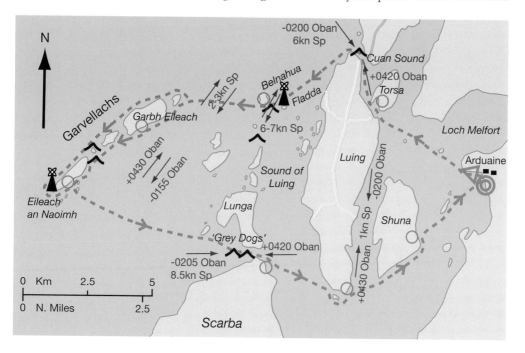

5

and the fantastic vista of what lies ahead will come into view. The dramatic fladda Lighthouse will be in the foreground, alongside the strangely shaped island of Belnahua. Beyond this you will see the elegant Garvellachs, with the imposing south coast of Mull behind. In addition there will be a maze of islands around Lunga with the larger islands of Scarba and Jura towering behind. This is the paddling playground for the rest of the journey, it is definitely the kind of playground where one visit will never be enough.

On reaching the strange-shaped slate island of Belnahua, head to the south end to pull ashore in the little natural slate bay. It is worth spending the time to explore this unique island that used to support a major slate quarrying industry. All that is left now are the obvious quarry scars along with the quarry workers' cottages and rusting machinery. Leaving Belnahua head across to the most northerly of the Garvellachs, Dun Chonnuill, where a castle used to stand on its green summit. Arriving at the Garvellachs it is easy to understand how they were once called 'Isles of the Sea' by Adomnan in early Gaelic. The biggest decision for the paddler now is whether to explore the steep cliffs of the west coast, or the sheltered interest of the east. Maybe the weather will decide for you, or maybe you will have to do both! If paddling down the east coast of Garbh Eileach you will pass the sheltered bay and well-kept house at Rubha Mor. The house is locked and used by the local shepherds when tending the sheep. Continuing on down through the Garvellachs be sure to look out for the natural arch on the north-western corner of Eileach an Naoimh. This island, whose name translates into 'rocky place of the saint', will be the end of the journey for the day and the sheltered natural bay by the old monastery on the east coast will be the best stopping place. It is this monastery that the Garvellachs are best known for, and to have the time to fully explore it is a fantastic opportunity. It dates from AD 542 when it was founded by St Brendan of Clonfert, the

uncle of St Columba, who founded the nowadays more famous monastery at Iona 21 years after St Brendan's monastery. St Columba is said to have often visited the Garvellachs monastery as a favourite place for peace and contemplation. Enjoy the peace on your visit as it is the perfect place to contemplate the paddling journey you have just done, and your prospects for the coming day.

The crossing next day will give fantastic views all around and the dramatic island of Scarba will draw you on. If it is clear the island of Colonsay 30km to the south will be visible. The narrow gap between Scarba and Lunga is the destination, and this is known as Bealach a Choin Ghlais, or more commonly used is its English translation, 'the Grey Dogs'. The tide rushes through this narrow gap, and for the paddler it provides a fun conveyor belt ride into the Sound of Luing, in the right conditions. After the excitement of the crossing and the Grey Dogs there is a resting place at Rubh a Chuil on Scarba, before the journey is continued. Crossing with the tidal streams to the south end of Luing will take you to the final leg of the journey along the shore of Shuna and on to Arduaine. There is another resting place at Poll na Gile on Shuna if required, but all too soon it will be journey's end and nothing but the memories left to savour.

Tide & Weather

To complete the trip out to the Garvellachs good weather conditions are required. If this is not possible, or the weather changes, then shelter can be found around the islands of Shuna, Luing and Lunga where good paddling is still available. With strong tidal streams in many areas of the trip be careful to note the wind direction; if it is blowing against the tidal streams this will produce considerably rougher conditions.

Campsite on Belnahua

To complete this trip careful tidal planning is required to ensure tidal stream assistance throughout. With this considered it is best to leave Arduaine so that Cuan Point is reached at the start of the south-going stream, about 2 hours before HW Oban. Allowing time for a brief stop on the trip, then leaving Arduaine at about 4 hours before HW Oban should work well. This will give tidal assistance for the entire day, including the crossing from Belnahua to the Garvellachs, however using a transit is advisable so as not to be moved too far south by the tidal stream.

On leaving the Garvellachs it is essential to have the south-going stream assisting you until the southern tip of Luing, in order to pass through the Grey Dogs and across the Sound of Luing. The south stream starts at about 1 hour and 55 minutes before HW Oban, so it is best to leave the Garvellachs no later than 2 hours after HW Oban to allow time to reach Luing. If it is possible to arrive at the south tip of Luing as the north stream starts, at about 4 hours and 30 minutes after HW Oban it will assist you up past Shuna. If the southern tip of Luing is arrived at before the north-going stream starts, it is no great concern as the southerly flow around Shuna is relatively weak. When crossing from the Garvellachs, and more importantly when crossing the sound of Luing, the use of a transit is required to ensure you are not moved too far south by the tidal stream.

Additional Information

If the weather or time does not allow for the trip described there are plenty of good variations in this area. It is also possible to launch at Cuan Sound and this can be a useful starting point for other possible routes.

North Lismore

No. 6 | Grade A | 16km | 5 Hours | OS Sheet 49 | Tidal Port Oban

Start	△ A828 Lay-by at Polanach (937505)
Finish	◎ A828 Lay-by at Polanach (937505)
HW/LW	HW/LW at Port Appin is around 5 minutes before Oban.
Tidal times	For the Sound of Shuna and between North Lismore and the mainland: The S going stream starts at about 15 mins before HW Oban. The N going stream starts at about 6 hrs after HW Oban.
Tidal rates	There are two areas on this trip where the tidal streams run fastest: In the Sound of Shuna the average spring rate can reach 1 knot. Between the north of Lismore and the mainland the average spring rate can reach 2 knots.
Coastguard	Clyde, tel:01475 729988, VHF Weather 0810 UT

Introduction

This trip offers wildlife, history, coastal paddling and crossings all in a very small area. Being sheltered from the ocean swell it can give a great day out when other venues would be too exposed.

For the sea kayaker new to tidal planning and paddling, it is the perfect trip to start gaining such experience.

Description

Putting in at the lay-by offers an easy carry down to the water with a straightforward launch spot from the stony beach. From here you can go straight down the Sound of Shuna, but leaving that to the end of the trip and going round the north end of Shuna Island is recommended if conditions allow. Here you will soon pass a shingle beach to land if needed, if not continue around the island keeping a watchful eye for otters, which are seen here. The island is now used to farm sheep, but nobody has lived in the farm since 1961. The ruined castle on the south end actually used to be a domestic tower house and was built near the end of the 16th Century.

Leaving Shuna a short crossing will take you to the skerries of Eilean Glas and Eilean Gainimh. It is well worth the journey to these skerries as there are plenty of common seals and bird life making them their homes. It is possible to land on the north-east end of Eilean Gainimh to take in the views and watch the wildlife. From here, head to the sheltered waters of Port Ramsay on the northern end of Lismore Island. This island is well populated and renowned for its lime-rich fertile land, leading to a great variety of plant life. Again there are plenty of opportunities to view the local wildlife including numerous seals, which live amongst the islands of Ramsay. There is plenty of evidence of the old lime workings in this area as well, with Port Ramsay being overlooked by two rows of lime-burners' cottages. Continue up the coastline to Eilean nan Caorach where the old lime kilns and quarrymen's cottages are worth a visit.

If time allows, cross to the mainland where there is the navigation light; here you will discover the small old cast-iron beacon up on the rocks, which was used prior to the modern day navigation light. Paddling back to the cars you will pass the impressive Castle Stalker. In this area you will have the beauty of the shallow water and a view of the seabed wildlife, along with a great view of the castle. The Stewarts of Appin built the castle in about 1500, and James IV used it as a hunting lodge before it fell into disrepair; nowadays it is fully restored. You will soon pass the fish farm in the Sound of Shuna with the fantastic view up Loch Linnhe to finish.

Tide & Weather

This area is well sheltered from any swell, however Loch Linnhe does tend to funnel the wind. Squalls often come down the loch from the surrounding high mountains. The inside of the islands usually offers sheltered water in most conditions, however on the outside of Shuna and out at the skerries a rough sea state can quickly build in the wind.

Other than between the islands off the north of Lismore, the tidal streams are generally unnoticeable. With this in mind it is possible to paddle the trip at any state of the tide. If best use of the tide is to be made then time it so as Port Ramsay is reached 5 hours after HW Oban. Starting the trip at 3-4 hours after HW Oban is ideal. This would give an hour's rest before leaving

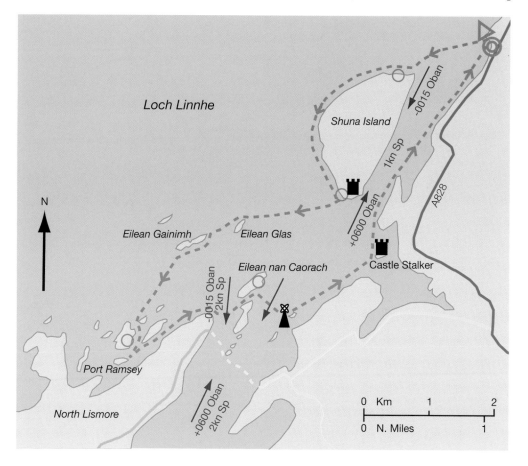

Castle Stalker

Port Ramsay about 6 hours after HW Oban to use the start of the north-going stream to finish the trip.

Additional Information

Port Appin has a hotel at the jetty if you need a place to eat. Alternatively the trip can be finished here if a shorter journey is wanted and a vehicle shuttle is possible. In the area around the north of Lismore care must be taken with the fast ferry boat which shuttles the workers to Glen Sanda quarry on the west side of Loch Linnhe.

Iona Abbey

Iona

No. 7 | Grade B | 18km | 5 Hours | OS Sheet 48 | Tidal Port Oban

Start	△ Kintra (314254)
Finish	◎ Kintra (314254)
HW/LW	HW/LW on Iona is about 5 mins before Oban.
Tidal times	In the Sound of Iona:
	The N going stream starts about 5 hrs and 15 mins after HW Oban. The S going stream starts about 15 mins before HW Oban.
	On the west side of Iona: The N going stream starts about 6 hrs after HW Oban. The S going stream starts about 15 minutes before HW Oban.
Tidal rates	In the Sound of Iona, the average spring rate is 2.5 knots.
	On the west side of Iona, the average spring rate is 1.5 knots.
Coastguard	Clyde, tel:01475 729988, VHF Weather 0810 UT

Introduction

This is a trip around a unique island with a special quality that attracts many pilgrims every year.

Iona village

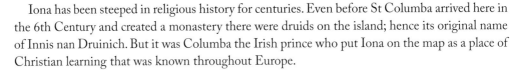

Iona has been steeped in religious history for centuries. Even before St Columba arrived here in the 6th Century and created a monastery there were druids on the island; hence its original name of Innis nan Druinich. But it was Columba the Irish prince who put Iona on the map as a place of Christian learning that was known throughout Europe.

Description

The very quiet surroundings of Kintra provide an ideal place to start this trip, away from the busy Fionnphort.

Head out from Kintra in a WNW direction and cross the north entrance to the Sound of Iona to reach Caolas Annraidh. Out to the north in the distance you might be able to see Staffa, and yet further, slightly to the left, the Treshnish Isles.

The beautiful white sandy beaches at the north end of Iona are backed by lovely machair, a rich pasture nourished by the seashells that have been deposited here over many thousands of years.

This north-west coast of Iona is very quiet, you probably won't see anyone until you reach Camas Cuil an t-Saimh with the golf course behind. South of the Spouting Cave keep an eye out for the semi-precious stone 'Serpentine' which can be found amongst the beach stones along this coast. Serpentine is a lovely green stone that is easy to work with due to its softness.

Port na Curaich on the south coast is recorded as the place where St Columba used to land on Iona when returning from Ireland. About 3kms SW from here is Soa Island, which translates to Sheep Island. Further up the east coast is another stunner of a beach, Traigh Mhor, a fine sheltered spot protected by the string of islets to the south.

Iona, being at the centre of learning, was the place to be buried if you were a king, 8 Norwegian, 4 Irish and 48 Scottish kings have been buried on Iona. At first thought, with modern day values, it is hard to understand why Iona was so central in years gone by, but just think in terms of sea transport and not road and it is easy to see how it could be a hub used by the Lord of the Isles in the 13th Century.

As with all places of importance many men lost their lives attacking or defending Iona and a short distance before the main jetty at Baile Mor is a small port where 60 to 70 monks were massacred in the distant past.

Visiting the Iona Abbey and the many other sites of interest on the island is most definitely worth doing, but these tourist traps are best visited on a separate trip. The magic qualities of a kayak trip round Iona should be continued undisturbed and passing through the ferry lane and onward to quieter shores will preserve the experience, whereas joining the hoards would potentially ruin an otherwise memorable trip.

Iona itself is a fertile island, due to the different rocks that are its foundation and the covering of shell sand that is rich in calcium, but across the sound on the Ross of Mull the ground is less fertile due to the acidic nature of the granite. The quality of the granite here is so good that it has been used to build lighthouses such as Skerryvore which lies 45km to the west of Iona.

Another plus side is the colour, the granite here is a striking pink. Combine this with the crystal clear waters, blue sky and white sand and you have a wonderful place to paddle through on your return to Kintra.

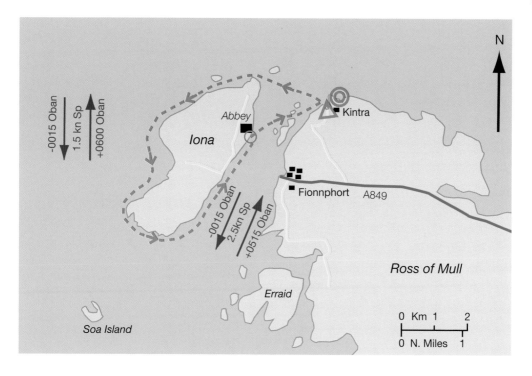

Abandoned marble quarry

Tide & Weather

The tides are not that strong, but going against the 3rd and 4th hours of the tide in the Sound of Iona could be somewhat tiresome. The south and west coast are exposed to the prevailing winds and swell, and therefore have scope to provide some rough water that might not be that apparent at Kintra where you put in. Plan to be at the south end of Iona when the north-going stream starts at about 5 hours 15 minutes after HW Oban. This will mean that you will have had the luxury of the tide pushing you down the west side of Iona and then when it turns it will convey you northward up the Sound of Iona. Leaving Kintra about 2 hours and 30 minutes earlier would make this possible.

Additional Information

The ferry that crosses from Fionnphort to Iona takes only passengers, no cars. There is also a ferry from here to the island of Staffa.

Treshnish and Staffa

No. 8 | **Grade C** | **Day 1 - 22km/6hrs** | **Day 2 - 30km/8hrs** | **OS Sheet 48** | **Tidal Port Oban**

Start	△ Ulva Ferry (446398)
Finish	◎ Ulva Ferry (446398)
HW/LW	HW/LW in Ulva Sound is about 10 minutes before Oban.
Tidal times	In the entire area: The N going stream starts about 5 hrs and 55 mins before HW Oban. The S going stream starts about 15 mins after HW Oban.
Tidal rates	There are two areas on this trip where there are tidal streams: In the area around Treshnish, Staffa and Ulva the average spring rate can reach 0.75 knots. In the area between N. Treshnish and Rubh a Chaoil the average spring rate can reach 2.5 knots.
Coastguard	Clyde, tel:01475 729988, VHF Weather 0810 UT

Introduction

This is a journey of quite magical qualities, and those who paddle it will want to stay for as long as possible. The Treshnish Isles are without doubt a green oasis in a turquoise sea that is dominated

by the wildlife, the king of which is the puffin. Across that turquoise sea is Staffa with its unique and spectacular cliffs guarding the cave of all caves, Fingal's. Sir Walter Scott, Jules Verne, Dr David Livingstone and Queen Victoria to name a few, have visited this island. It inspired them all, and it will most certainly inspire you as well.

Description

The slipway of the Ulva Ferry is the starting point, and from this sheltered launch you head into the sound of Ulva. While paddling through the sound and around the north side of the island of Ulva, it is hard to believe that this was the site of a drowning due to love many years ago. It is said that Lord Ullin was chasing his daughter who was eloping with the Chief of Ulva; it was a stormy night and the Chief persuaded the boatman to cross the sound back to Ulva to escape Lord Ullin's fury. Tragically the boat with its cargo of two lovers never made it to Ulva and they were all drowned. They are said to be buried on the Mull shore near to the Ulva Ferry.

As you paddle along the coastline of Ulva it is apparent why it is designated an Area of Outstanding Natural Beauty, and you may well see otters playing and deer grazing on the shore. In the early 1800's Ulva and Gometra supported over 800 people, and it is said that every family owned at least one boat and there was more food produced than the island needed. Having explored the Ulva coastline it is worth stopping at Eilean Dioghlum, before the crossing to the Treshnish Isles. This is an ideal place to stretch the legs as, from the top of the island you are rewarded with a fantastic view of what is to come.

The crossing to the Treshnish Isles with the afternoon sun in your face and the sea glistening all around is enough to inspire any paddler. Head across to the conspicuous two northerly islands

of Cairn na Burgh More and Beg. Each of these two dramatic outcrops of rock house what must be one of the most impenetrable castles around? The castle on the larger of the islands dates back to Norse times when there was a fort evident. On the smaller island the castle is said to have been built in the 1700's and used during the Jacobite rising. Beside the castle remains on the larger island, Cairn na Burgh More, there is also evidence of a small chapel. On leaving these islands head down past Fladda and the mass of skerries that lead you to the largest of the islands, Lunga.

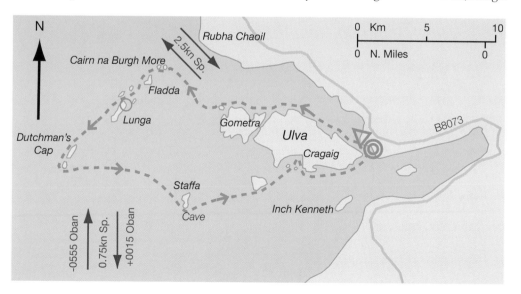

Although a short distance this will undoubtedly take a surprising amount of time, due to travelling slowly and viewing the amazing amount of marine and bird life that these island have. Landing on the north tip of Lunga will provide an ideal campsite for the night, and it is well worth stopping to allow time to explore the island. Here you will discover the remains of the black houses on the island, which housed up to twenty people until 1824. Walking around Lunga you will soon fall in love with its magical feel, surrounded by a colourful sea and the island's natural beauty. You will be sharing the island with its main occupants today, puffins. So enjoy the company and close up viewings you will have of the comical birds; doing this trip in the spring and early summer is recommended in order to see them.

The next day's paddling down by the cliffs off the west side of Lunga will take you ever closer to the unique volcanic cone of the Dutchman's Cap. If time allows it is well worth exploring this southerly island of the Treshnish Isles before heading across to the most famous rocky island of them all, Staffa. Throughout the 8km crossing the dramatic basalt cliffs of Staffa will draw you on, gradually revealing more and more of their grandeur. On arriving at the west coast of this island, head around to the southern end where the famous cliffs and caves can be explored. The symmetry of these basalt columns is a natural wonder; they were formed by lava from a volcanic eruption cooling rapidly on contact with sea water millions of years ago, and are similar in appearance to the Giant's Causeway rock formations in Northern Ireland. You will paddle under the 'Great Face' and if conditions allow be able to explore the immense and spectacular Boat Cave, Fingal's Cave and Clamshell Cave, with others alongside. There is an easy pebble beach landing on the east coast of the island that gives the opportunity to join the summer tourists and explore Fingal's Cave on foot as well.

Puffins

It has to be hard not to fall in love with puffins, and along the Scottish coastline we are lucky to have some of Britain's main breeding colonies. Close up they are easily recognisable by their bright yellow, red and white striped beaks, and for this reason they are also sometimes called 'sea parrots'. From a distance they can still be recognised by their very fast wing beats as they skim the sea's surface. These birds spend their lives at sea, only coming to land between April and mid-August to breed. Living the rest of the time far out at sea in all conditions make them remarkably tough creatures. They are able to swim exceptionally well, feeding on fish and drinking the salt water. When breeding they live in burrows, which are excavated in the soil, found on top of the coastal cliffs. Puffins choose partners for life and each year will incubate one egg, returning to the same burrow annually. After hatching, the young will spend about 45 days in the burrow before it heads out to sea to begin its life. It will spend two to three years at sea before returning to the same breeding area to start a family of its own.

Leaving Staffa it is time to head for Little Colonsay and Ulva on the return journey to Ulva Ferry slipway. If time allows or an extra day is taken, then these islands have an interesting coastline to explore as well. The wildlife does not give up and the natural beauty continues. The sheltered bay of Cragaig is well worth visiting with its ruined watermill and black house to explore. Continuing along the coastline will soon lead you back into the Ulva Sound and storms, lovers and angry fathers permitting, this will be the finish of a fantastic journey.

Guillemots nesting on Lunga

Tide & Weather

The Treshnish Isles are exposed to weather from all directions, and with this in mind, reasonable conditions are best. To make the most of this trip and be able to enjoy the caves of Staffa, it is best to wait for perfect conditions.

The tidal streams throughout the journey are relatively weak, and are generally paddled across. So the tidal planning is not too important, however there will be tidal movement around Cairn na Burgh More and Beg where it can reach a speed of 2.5 knots, so be aware of this. If it is possible to arrive at these northernmost islands at the start of the south-going stream, 15 minutes after HW Oban, this will be best, but not essential.

Additional Information

There are regular summer tourist boats out to Staffa and the Treshnish Isles, so do not expect complete solitude for the journey. There is a visitor centre and restaurant above the ferry at Ulva, and a telephone box can be found there, as well as on the main road to the Ulva Ferry. The island of Staffa is owned by the National Trust for Scotland and is one of Scotland's National Nature Reserves (NNR's), visit www.nts.org.uk for more information. For further details about all of Scotland's NNR's visit the Scottish Natural Heritage website, www.snh.org.uk.

Ulva Ferry can be busy in summer months with limited private parking. Please use the car park 250m on the right prior to the ferry. For further information please go to www.ulva.mull.com.

Ardnamurchan Point

No. 9 | **Grade C** | **14km** | **4 Hours** | **OS Sheet 47** | **Tidal Port Oban**

Start	△ Kilchoan (480636)
Finish	◎ Portuairk (Sanna Bay) (435684)
HW/LW	HW/LW at Tobermory is about 20 minutes after Oban.
Tidal times	Off the Point of Ardnamurchan: The NE going stream starts about 5 hrs 25 mins before HW Oban. The SW going stream starts about 1 hr after HW Oban.
Tidal rates	Off the Point of Ardnamurchan the average spring rate is 1.5 knots.
Coastguard	Clyde, tel:01475 729988, VHF Weather 0810 UT

Introduction

This headland is the most westerly point on the Scottish mainland. For those who sail it marks a change between southern waters with many sheltered anchorages that are easy to get into, and a coastline that is altogether more dramatic.

It is a stunning view from the lighthouse at the Point of Ardnamurchan. To the south is Mull, to the south-west is Coll, and to the north are Muck, Eigg and Rum, known collectively with Canna as the Small Isles.

So renowned is the challenge of getting past the Point of Ardnamurchan that tradition amongst seafaring folk allows those who pass safely to display a sprig of lucky white heather on their craft.

Description

Kilchoan is the main village on the Ardnamurchan peninsula, but there is not a lot to it! Fortunately it does have a petrol station and a shop where you can buy general provisions.

Apart from the ferry going across to Tobermory you might also see the ferry from Oban going to or returning from Castlebay on Barra, the most southerly port in the Outer Hebrides.

Once past Sron Bheag the view opens out a bit and the northern part of the island of Coll can be seen. Coll is one of the sunniest places in the UK, and has a strange claim to fame of trying to grow tulips for the cut flower trade. Apparently due to the very fertile machair and mild climate, the tulips flourished, but due to the high cost of transporting the flowers from the island it was never going to be big business.

The coastline gets rougher the closer you get to the lighthouse, the steep hillsides with many outcrops and cliffs are heather-clad for the most part. A closer look will reveal trees growing not so much upright, but very close to the ground, appearing shrub-like. The stunted, creeping nature of the trees is due to the exposure this headland experiences, strong winds and salt spray do all they can to restrict growth.

There is little chance of landing until you are past the lighthouse where one kilometre to the east there is a little bay (423673).

The lighthouse is built with the pink granite from the Ross of Mull and is another of the many lights built by the famous Stevenson family. There is a museum at the lighthouse, so if you can land in the little bay it is worth the walk up to the light for the view and a look around the museum.

In Sanna Bay, Portuairk provides a landing spot where the carry is not too long; over at Sanna in the NE corner of the bay it is harder to get a car close to the water.

In the little sheltered bays around Portuairk there are often many cowries to be found. These are little pink shells around 1cm long with a rounded back that sometimes sports three dark spots and ridges and grooves running across the ridge, with a long slit opening on the underside.

Tide & Weather

Fully exposed to the prevailing swell and winds from the SW, the Point of Ardnamurchan can provide a bumpy ride. It is not unusual to experience quite a bit of clapotis on the coast south of the lighthouse.

When the SW stream is running it can create a bit of an eddy south of the lighthouse, where you might experience a NW flow parallel with the coast. Leaving Kilchoan about 1 hour and 30 minutes before HW Oban should give you time enough to arrive at the Point of Ardnamurchan in the last hour of the NE stream, and before the SW stream starts.

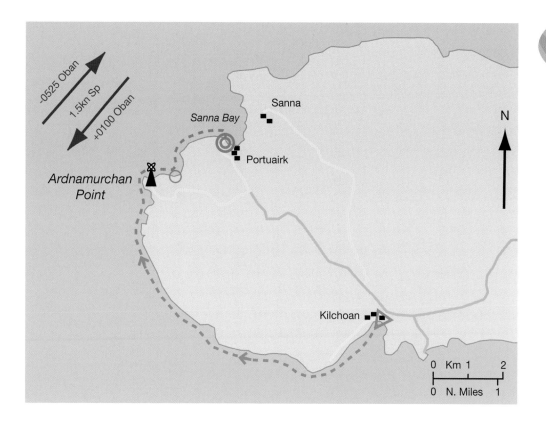

Looking SW towards Coll

Additional Information

If you want to extend the trip along the north coast of the peninsula it is worth noting that there is no vehicular access to Fascadale (500707) and it is a bit of a walk down to Port Ban (517704) and Kilmory Bay (524705).

Portuairk is a good place from which to do a day trip out to the Isle of Muck, about 11km to the north.

Arisaig

No. 10 | Grade A | 11km | 3 Hours | OS Sheet 40 | Tidal Port Ullapool

Start	△ Gortenachullish (642877) or
	Road head by South Channel, Loch nan Ceall (627852)
Finish	◎ Arisaig (657865)
HW/LW	HW/LW at Arisaig is around 40 minutes before Ullapool.
Tidal times	For Loch nan Ceall:
	The ingoing stream starts about 5 hrs and 45 mins after HW Ullapool.
	The outgoing stream starts at about 50 mins before HW Ullapool.
Tidal rates	In the N and S Channels the average spring rate can reach 1-2 knots.
Coastguard	Stornoway, tel:01851 702013, VHF Weather 0710 UT

Introduction

This area is the nearest you will get to paddling in the Caribbean in Scotland. On a sunny day it has golden sands and crystal clear waters with the seabed visible as you paddle over. The wildlife is stunning, with hundreds of inquisitive common seals around, in amongst the calls of a great variety of birds. Add to this the backdrop of the isles of Rum, Eigg, Muck and Skye and it is a truly magical place.

Description

   Just before reaching the campsite at the end of the road at Gortenachullish there is a perfect little sheltered sandy bay, which marks the start of our trip. Parking is on the grass verge and is limited so please be considerate. At low tide launching here can require a few hundred metres of carrying over the sand, but it is easy walking. On leaving the bay you are instantly provided with a perfect view of the Cuillin Mountains on Skye, whilst the water is shallow enough for a perfect view of the seabed habitat. Paddle out around Eilean Ighe; the passage separating this island and the mainland is rarely navigable. The outside of Eilean Ighe provides the most exposed bit of water of our trip; if this is not to your liking then starting at the road head by the South Channel in Loch nan Ceall (627852) provides more shelter. With this exposure to the ocean comes breathtaking views of the mountains of Rum, the distinctive An Sgurr peak on Eigg, and Muck is just visible to the south. Cross the North Channel heading for the main inlet amongst the mass of skerries just to the east of Luinga Bheag. As you make your way from here to Luinga Mhor you will be passing through a wildlife haven. There will be common seals all around inquisitively checking you out and following where you go. Around the seals there will be oystercatchers and curlews to name a few of the birds to be seen. It is the kind of environment you could lose yourself in for hours watching the wildlife, with the constant backdrop of beaches and mountains. Luinga Mhor provides a good stopping place, with a choice of small areas of beach on its eastern side to land.

   After a rest continue exploring the waters around this unique area of skerries and beaches as you make your way to Sgeir Ghainmheach, the innermost large skerry. A gentle paddle back into the pretty village of Arisaig will take you past yet more seals and wildlife if you keep to the northern

Common Seal

The common seal, or harbour seal as it is also known, is found in many areas of Scotland and is one of only two species of seal found regularly in the UK. Although called the common seal there are in fact more grey seals in Scotland. The common seal is seen throughout Scotland, but are most regularly seen along the more sheltered mainland coastlines. They are recognisable from a grey seal in a number of ways: they are smaller (average male 1.5m in length), their faces are more 'dog' shaped and their colour is more varied (often mottled with spots and rings). The common seals give birth in late June and early July, with the young being able to swim with their mothers within a few hours. The pup will be suckled for up to six weeks and then if lucky to survive this vulnerable period, go on to live up to 40 years. The common seals can dive down to 200m in depth for periods up to fifteen minutes. When hunting they swim up to 20 knots, although will generally cruise at about 2 or 3 knots.

side of the loch. In Arisaig there are plenty of places to land, either the marina or beach, and parking is not a problem. At low water the marina is better. If a shuttle has not been possible, then to return to the start from Sgeir Ghainmheach will be a similar distance as finishing in Arisaig.

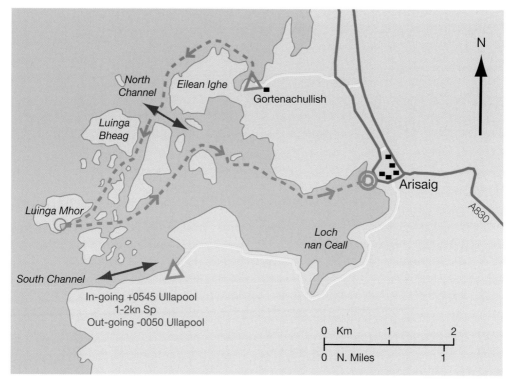

Looking over Arisaig skerries to Skye

Tide & Weather

Loch nan Ceall and the skerries provide a lot of shelter in most weather conditions and is therefore a great venue to visit. It can be rough on the outside of the skerries and island with both swell and wind, so care should be taken if less experienced in these conditions.

The tidal streams are only really noticeable in the narrows of the North and South Channels, and are therefore always avoidable by eddy hopping amongst the skerries. At their fastest though it is still possible to paddle against them in the narrows.

To make best use of any tidal movement and avoid long carries at the launching and landing, starting 4 hours before HW Ullapool works well. For launching this will mean the tide is about halfway in, and for landing at the end of the trip it will be around high water. It will also mean that you will have about the last three hours of the ingoing stream to help you on your way towards Arisaig when paddling through the North and South Channels.

Additional Information

Arisaig is well serviced with shops and a hotel. Boats and a ferry use both North and South Channels, so care should be taken when paddling in these areas. The marina is happy for kayaks to launch and land, but please ask for permission and park considerately.

Eigg and Muck from Arisaig

11

No. 11 | Grade C | Day 1 - 22km/6-7hrs | Day 2 - 30km/8hrs | Day 3 - 17km/4-5hrs | OS Sheets 39 & 40 | Tidal Port Ullapool

Start	△ Road head by South Channel, Loch nan Ceall (627852)
Finish	◎ Road head by South Channel, Loch nan Ceall (627852)
HW/LW	HW/LW at Bay of Laig, Eigg and Arisaig is about 40 minutes before Ullapool.
Tidal times	For Loch nan Ceall: The ingoing stream starts about 5 hrs and 45 mins after HW Ullapool. The outgoing stream starts about 50 mins before HW Ullapool.
	Between Eigg and the mainland: The N going stream starts about 5 hrs and 50 mins after HW Ullapool. The S going stream starts about 10 mins before HW Ullapool.
	Around Eigg and Muck: The N going stream starts about 6 hours after HW Ullapool. The S going stream starts about HW Ullapool.
Tidal rates	There are four areas on this trip where the tidal streams run at their fastest: In Loch nan Ceall North and South Channels the average spring rate can reach 1-2 knots.

Off the east coast of Eigg the average spring rate can reach 4 knots.
In the Sound of Eigg the average spring rate can reach 3 knots.
Off the east and west coasts of Muck the average spring rate can reach 4 knots.

Coastguard   Stornoway, tel:01851 702013, VHF Weather 0710 UT

Introduction

To leave the shelter of Loch nan Ceall and head off on a journey that takes you across to the 'Small Isles' is a must for any paddler. If you only have a few days then this is a great trip, if you have longer then taking in Rum and Canna is a good idea. This trip has big open crossings, rugged exposed coastlines, beautiful sandy beaches and palm trees, to highlight just a few of the attractions. An area where whales and marine wildlife are often seen, it is a journey that will definitely leave long-lasting memories.

Description

Setting off amongst the mass of small skerries as you leave Loch nan Ceall provides a wildlife oasis with golden sands all around. Try not to delay too long in this area as Eigg beckons. Once you leave these skerries it is a 12km open crossing that takes you across to Eigg. With the imposing Sgurr of Eigg leading you on and the views of Skye, Rum and Muck all around there is plenty to take the mind off the crossing. There are regular sightings of whales in this area as well, so keep an ever-watchful eye and ear for these fantastic creatures of the ocean. Head for the sandy beach

(Poll nam Partan) below the old ruined fort, south of Kildonnan as your first landing spot on Eigg. While stretching your legs after the crossing you may wish to discover the old Celtic cross-slab and ruined church at Kildonnan. It is said that St Donan set up a monastery here with fifty-two of his monks, who in 617 were all murdered by either pirates or warrior women who apparently had a disliking for missionaries. Eigg's more recent history is also of note as it was one of the first islands to have a community buy out, it now being owned and run by the people who live there.

From here, head up the remote east coast to the northern tip of Eigg. If you have time, you may wish to stop and explore Eilean Thuilm for fossils which have been found in the rocks of this area. Continuing on around the next headland you will start to get a feel for the more rugged west coast of Eigg as you reach the fantastic beach of Camas Sgiotaig. This is also known as the 'singing sands' as the dry grains of quartz drone underfoot or sing when the wind blows across them. The area of grass behind the beach makes a fantastic campsite, with a wonderful view north-westward to Rum. It is well worth spending the night here to watch the sun set behind the mountains of Rum and then again watch the early morning light bathe these shapely Norse named mountains the next day.

Surf can often come into this beach, so there is every chance of an early morning wake up shower when leaving to continue the journey. As you cross the Bay of Laig you will reach the most exposed, yet spectacular, part of the trip. This bit of coastline down to the south of Eigg is fully exposed to the westerly seas, has no landings and is lined by steep cliffs along the entire route. If conditions allow then there will also be a chance to explore the odd cave and go in amongst the cliffs to enjoy the varied bird life that uses this part of Eigg for their summer home. On reaching the southern coastline, Muck will be beckoning and the sandy beach at Gallanach is the place to head for. This provides an idyllic resting place to relax and enjoy after the 12km journey from last night's campsite.

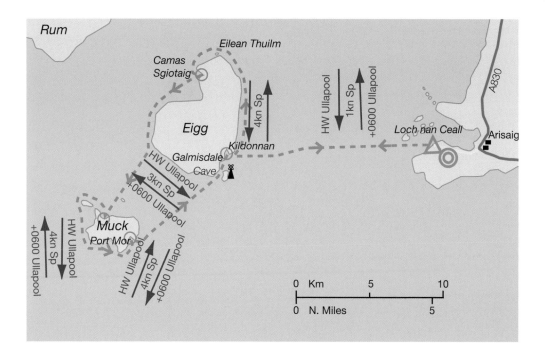

On leaving the sandy beaches head out around the west coast of Muck and enjoy the wildness of this island while heading for the next easy landing place at Port Mor. Muck in Gaelic translates into the 'Isle of Pigs', which could have come from the fact that porpoises were known as sea pigs and are often seen playing in these waters. Port Mor is the main centre for Muck and is where the small school is situated, along with a café for the weary paddler. It is possible to camp here, or once fuelled up from the café, make the crossing back to Eigg to spend the second night. If continuing to Eigg head for Galmisdale, and you will find somewhere to camp in this area.

Before leaving Galmisdale and crossing back to Arisaig you may want to walk and find the caves of Uamh Fhraing. It is here in 1577 that 195 Eigg islanders hid from the MacLeods from Skye. The MacLeods were on the island to retaliate after some of them had been sent back to Skye castrated after being caught raping some MacDonald girls on Eigg. The Macleods found the 195 hidden islanders and, in smoking them out of the cave, it is said that all the islanders were suffocated. For this reason the cave is known as 'Massacre Cave'.

With the memories of the previous two days' paddling exploring these unique islands, the crossing back to the skerries of Loch nan Ceall will soon pass. It is with tired bodies, yet fulfilled souls that you will reach the cars and tourists of the mainland.

Tide & Weather

Due to the long crossings, exposed coastlines and few landings good weather will be required to complete this trip. If the weather changes, then shelter is never too far away amongst the islands, the west coast of Eigg and the mainland crossing being the most weather dependant sections.

Whales

If lucky, a variety of whales can be seen in British waters, and the remote areas of Scotland's west and north coasts are ideal for whale spotting. Killer, sperm, pilot, humpback, bottlenosed and minke whale have all been seen around these coastlines. Of these whales there is only one that is seen fairly regularly and that is the minke whale. Unlike dolphins and porpoises they do not have teeth, but instead have horny plates that hang down from the animal's palate. These can strain the tiny animals and small fish that they feed on, and due to this they fit into the group of whales known as baleen whales. The minke whale grows up to 10m long, with a relatively tall dorsal fin set two-thirds of the way down its back. They are dark slate grey in colour with paler grey to white undersides and throat, their flippers having a distinctive white band. Seen individually or in groups of two or three they are very inquisitive, often first noticed when they blow water 2 to 3m in the air out of their blowholes. These whales will often live to be about 60 years old.

To make best use of the tides, time leaving Arisaig so that you reach Eigg when the north-going stream has started, about 6 hours after HW Ullapool. On the crossing there is no more than about 1 knot of north/south tidal stream at springs. Despite this the use of a transit will be ideal to ensure an efficient crossing. To get to Eilean Thuilm you will have the north-going stream to assist. On leaving Camas Sgiotaig, time it so that the south-going stream will be assisting you on the journey to Muck, this starts at about HW Ullapool. Leaving camp at 3 hours after HW Ullapool

East coast of Muck

will get you to Muck for 6 hours after HW Ullapool. This will give slacker water to circumnavigate Muck, as well as the first and last hours of the tide to cross the Sound of Eigg. In the Sound of Eigg the tidal streams run either north-west or south-east, and therefore transits should again be used on the crossing. The north-going stream is then going to assist you paddling back to Eigg.

In the North and South Channels in Loch nan Ceall, this can also be timed to have tidal assistance, however if this does not fit in with the times for arriving/leaving Eigg then these streams are short-lived and easily paddled against, especially if eddies are used between prominent points.

Additional Information

In Arisaig there are a full range of local amenities. There are summer ferry services running to and from Eigg and Muck from Mallaig. You can carry your kayak on board this service and it will make it possible to explore the islands without paddling the open crossing from the mainland. You may also want to consider linking this trip with Trip 12: Rum and Canna, and catching the ferry back from either of these islands. For further information on ferry times contact Caledonian MacBrayne Ferries on www.calmac.uk. There are limited amenities on the islands, however they are serviced with small shops and a telephone box on Muck at Port Mor.

Rum and Canna

No. 12 | **Grade C** | **Day 1 - 33km/8hrs** | **Day 2 - 26km/6-7hrs** | **Day 3 - 34km/8hrs** | **OS Sheet 32/39** | **Tidal Port Ullapool**

Start	△ Glen Brittle (410205)
Finish	◎ Glen Brittle (410205)
HW/LW	HW/LW on Rum and Canna is about 50 minutes before Ullapool.
Tidal times	For the SE and SW coast of Rum:

For the SE and SW coast of Rum:
The N going stream starts about 5 hrs and 50 mins after HW Ullapool.
The S going stream starts at about 10 mins before HW Ullapool.

In the Sound of Canna:
The NE going stream starts about 6 hrs after HW Ullapool.
The SW going stream starts about HW Ullapool.

Off the west coast of Canna:
The N going stream starts about 6 hrs and 15 mins after HW Ullapool.
The S going stream starts about 15 mins after HW Ullapool.

Tidal rates   There are five areas on this trip where the tidal streams run fastest:
Along the SE coast of Rum the average spring rate can reach 3 knots.
Along the SW coast of Rum the average spring rate can reach 3 knots.
In the Sound of Canna the average spring rate can reach 1.5 knots.

Cliffs on west coast of Canna

Off the east coast of Sanday the average spring rate can reach 4-5 knots.
Off the west coast of Canna the average spring rate can reach 2.5 knots.

Coastguard   Stornoway, tel:01851 702013, VHF Weather 0710 UT

Introduction

This is an outstanding sea kayak trip that has everything a kayaker could ask for. In the right conditions it provides fantastic cliffs, towering mountains and plentiful wildlife. There is a real sense of remoteness on the committing coastlines and crossings, where the passing whales and sea eagles will be the only company.

Description

Starting from Glen Brittle on the Isle of Skye provides the shortest crossing distance to these islands, but this being 12km it is not to be undertaken lightly. A last-minute leg stretch is available at Rubh' an Dunain before you leave Skye and head to the beaches and mountains of Rum. To do this crossing on a calm day is best not only for ease of paddling, but also as you are more likely to see the minke whales and porpoises which are found in this area. Kayak over to the headland of Rubha Shamhnan Insir which has a fantastic beach just to the east; this is a superb place to relax and enjoy your first taste of Rum. The island is a National Nature Reserve, National Scenic Area, a Site of Special Scientific Interest, a Biosphere Reserve and a Specially Protected Area, but you will not need these titles to quickly realise it is a unique place to visit. The island is now owned and managed by Scottish Natural Heritage (SNH) who both conserve and study the natural and cultural history of the island. If time is on your side you may wish to while away the rest of the day on the fantastic beach. If however you are on a three day timescale the journey must continue.

Paddling on down the east coast you will pass a few smaller beaches before reaching the tree-lined shores of Loch Scresort. The main inhabitation on the island as well as the pier is found at the head of this loch, this being Kinloch. It is mainly SNH workers and visitors who live here, but if time allows you may want to take the opportunity to visit. Even if you choose not to land, ensure that you see the incredible Kinloch Castle. This castle has a peculiar history to it and was built in 1902 by George Bullough whose family owned the island from 1888 until 1957 when they sold it to the Nature Conservancy Council for £26,000. Having inherited the island from his father George Bullough built the castle after sailing around the world. Money was no object to him and

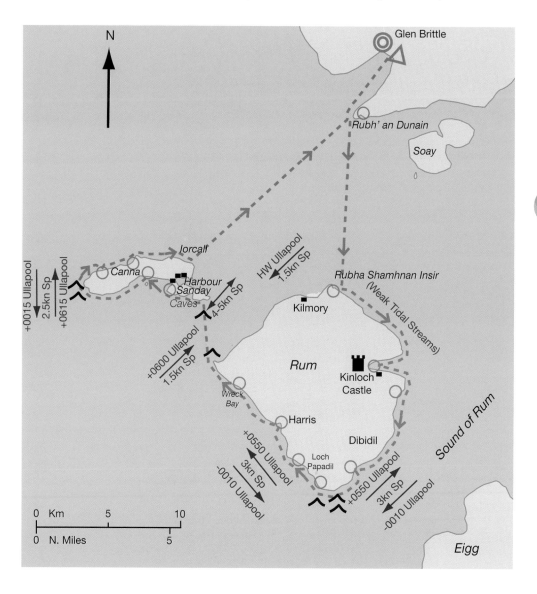

he imported a workforce and materials from all over the UK in order to build his dream castle. The finished castle is a sight to behold and in its day housed air conditioning in the billiard hall, a Victorian 'jacuzzi' bath, birds of paradise in the conservatory and live turtles and alligators in heated tanks! George Bullough's guests were brought to Mallaig by private train, taken by steam yacht to the island where they were met by Albion motorcars, which were kept on the island. Nowadays SNH unfortunately do not have the same wealth as George Bullough for the upkeep of the castle and it is past its best. It appeared as part of a television series called 'Restoration', in which viewers could vote for featured historical buildings from around the UK to be renovated. Unfortunately although Kinloch Castle made the final it did not win, but hopefully the publicity has helped it in its plight. Leaving Loch Scresort, the view of Eigg will become ever more imposing and the distant Muck will draw closer. Glen Dibidil provides a fantastically remote campsite in the heart of the Cuillin Mountains of Rum, in which to spend a well-earned restful night after a big day's paddle. There is plenty of water, reasonable places for tents and a bothy if needed.

Leaving the sheltered waters of the east coast in order to head up the west coast of Rum and on to Canna is as committing a day's paddle as you could ask for. Paddling around the southern tip of Rum the cliffs will increase in size, the nesting birds will be screeching their warnings to you and the sea will come alive with the ocean swell. On a calm day you may be able to land for a rest at Loch Papadil, a beautifully situated freshwater loch where George Bullough built a lodge for his wife Lady Monica Bullough. She unfortunately did not like it and it is now just a ruin. Inbhir Ghil and Wreck Bay are two other possible landing places, but only on calm days otherwise your kayak may join the 'wrecks' on this section of coast. The bay at Harris is the only definite landing place, and with its sandy beach will be possible in rougher conditions. This is a beautiful location looking

Harris Beach, Rum

up to the mountains, with only the feral goats for company. It is also the site of the Bullough Mausoleum; looking like a Greek temple it was designed by George Bullough and it houses his father's, wife's and own tombs. On reaching A'Bhrideanach, the most westerly point of the island, it will be time to leave Rum and head for Canna. Hopefully you will have been lucky enough to see a white-tailed sea eagle. These magnificent birds were successfully reintroduced to Scotland in the 1970's with young birds brought over from Norway and released on Rum. If not, keep looking as they are often seen on Canna now as well.

The shortest crossing of the Sound of Canna is to the western tip of Sanday. This is well worth doing as there are some great caves on the southern side of Sanday as you head west along the coast to Canna. There is limited water on Canna, so hopefully you will have filled up on Rum. If not, or you have time to visit, you may wish to call in at the village on Canna. This offers camping with use of the farmhouse's toilets etc, a café/restaurant and water at the pier. If time does not allow, or you are keen to continue the wilderness feel of the trip then there is good camping at a small sandy beach on the south side of Canna north of the Haslam skerry (253053). If the weather is looking good and the energy levels are sufficient, you may consider continuing around the western point of Canna. If this is done there is another sandy beach and campsite just past Sgeir nan Sgarbh (220060).

While paddling around the western tip of Canna you will sense a fantastic feeling of remoteness, with dramatic cliffs and distant views to the Outer Hebrides to the north and west, and the light of Oigh-sgeir to the south-west. It was here that the cattle from Canna used to be taken out to for grazing; being 10km away from Canna this must have been quite a challenge. There is a possible stony landing place at Camas Thairbearnais on a calm day, but other than this there is little shelter for the kayaker on this coast. There is plenty of wildlife for company however, with grey seals, puffins and plenty of other seabirds all making this remote coastline their home. Be sure to have seen the sea stack of Iorcail and the nesting puffins on An t-Each, before making the 15km crossing back to Rubh' an Dunain and then into Loch Brittle. Whether the trip is completed in three days or three weeks, it will be guaranteed to leave lasting memories and a wish to return to explore more.

Tide & Weather

Due to the committing nature of this trip a period of settled weather will be required to make it possible. Off the southern and western coasts of Rum, Sound of Canna and west coast of Canna the tides can run up to 3 knots, this coupled with their exposed locations can give rough water.

To gain the most assistance from the tides it is best to time the trip so that the east coast of Rum is paddled on a south-west going stream, which starts 10 minutes after HW Ullapool. To reach the southern tip of Rum at the start of the north-east going stream, 5 hours and 50 minutes after HW Ullapool, will provide the calmest conditions and easiest paddling. This will then give tidal assistance until Canna, and then on around the west coast of Canna if this is paddled on the same day. If the west coast of Canna is paddled the next day, the north-going stream starts 15 minutes after HW Ullapool until 6 hours and 15 minutes after HW Ullapool, and it is best to paddle around this bit of coastline with this tide helping. On the crossings to and from Skye there is negligible tidal movement, and any wind will have a far greater effect. When crossing the Sound of Canna the tide runs considerably faster off the eastern tip of Sanday. With this considered, aim south-west of Sanday to compensate, using transits during the crossing.

Additional Information

For further information about Rum visit Scottish Natural Heritage's website, www.snh.org.uk. It is also possible to catch the ferry from Mallaig out to Rum and Canna taking kayaks on by hand. This can give more flexibility with the weather, and give an option of avoiding the crossing from Skye. In a similar amount of time it also gives the possibility of linking this trip with Trip 11: Eigg and Muck, by catching the ferry to Canna and back from Muck. For information on the ferries contact Caledonian MacBrayne Ferries on www.calmac.co.uk.

Rum and Canna

Loch Coruisk and Soay

No. 13 | Grade B | 30km | 7-8 Hours | OS Sheet 32 | Tidal Port Ullapool

Start	△ Elgol (516136)
Finish	◎ Elgol (516136)
HW/LW	HW/LW at Loch Scavaig is about 40 minutes before Ullapool.
Tidal times	For Loch Scavaig: The ingoing stream starts at about 5 hrs and 35 mins after HW Ullapool. The outgoing stream starts at about 25 mins before HW Ullapool. For Soay Sound: The W going stream flows continuously.
Tidal rates	In both the above areas the streams are weak, not exceeding 1 knot.
Coastguard	Stornoway, tel:01851 702013, VHF Weather 0710 UT

Introduction

In the shadow of the Black Cuillin Mountains of Skye, this journey has incredible mountain scenery on one side and a backdrop of the sea leading to the Small Isles on the other. It is also a trip

with the unique history of a shark fishery, along with plenty of wildlife. For a small area there is an unrivalled amount of variety and interest making it a great day out, or longer if time permits.

Description

Leaving the small fishing village of Elgol, it is best to head towards the lure of the Cuillin Mountains, into Loch Scavaig. These mountains are the most dramatic in the British Isles, forming a 12 mile long, knife-edge ridge that is the aspiration of many a mountaineer. Nestled into the remote and inaccessible eastern side of these great mountains is the dramatic setting for Loch Coruisk. It is the outflow from this loch where we are heading, into the inner sanctuary of Loch Scavaig. Paddling up the coastline into Loch Scavaig the bay of Camasunary is soon reached, which you may well paddle across. There is a beautifully situated bothy (Camasunary Bothy) on the shores of this bay if time allows for a visit. Soon the head of Loch Scavaig is reached, which is split into two lochs, Loch nan Leachd and Loch na Cuilce. You will be paddling amongst the guardians of this loch, the numerous common seals. There may well be yachts moored here as well with it being such a perfect anchorage with a five star view. Finding a landing spot just to the west of the Scavaig River will see you coming ashore by a solid looking little climbing hut, sporting the St Andrews cross, which is painted onto the window shutters. The Scottish Mountaineering Club owns the hut, which is for the use of its members and those of kindred mountaineering clubs, and unlike many bothies in Scotland it is kept locked when not in use. It is well worth stretching the legs by walking the very short distance up to Loch Coruisk, where the view into the heart of the Cuillins is breathtaking. It may well be hard to move on from this spot with the seals and other wildlife all around, views out to sea and an amphitheatre of mountains surrounding you. It is worth the effort to leave though as there is more to the journey yet.

Head out of Loch na Cuilce on the western coastline that leads around into Soay Sound. Cross the sound to reach the island of Soay and continue along the northern coastline into the perfectly formed and sheltered natural Soay Harbour. It is at the back of this you will find the factory ruins, once used by the Island of Soay Shark Fisheries. This was set up by the author Gavin Maxwell when he bought the island in 1946. The island was used as a base for the hunting of basking sharks that used to more regularly frequent these west coast waters, although it is good to hear that their numbers are now increasing again. The factory on the island was used to process the shark oil, although the venture only ran for three years due to the drop in value of shark oil in 1949. 'Tex' Geddes, who was the harpooner from the shark fishing days, owned the island prior to his death. From the back of the harbour there is a good path leading across the short gap to the bay of Camas nan Gall and the main village on the island. Although sparsely populated these days this village used to house 158 people at its busiest before the Clearances. On route to the village you will also

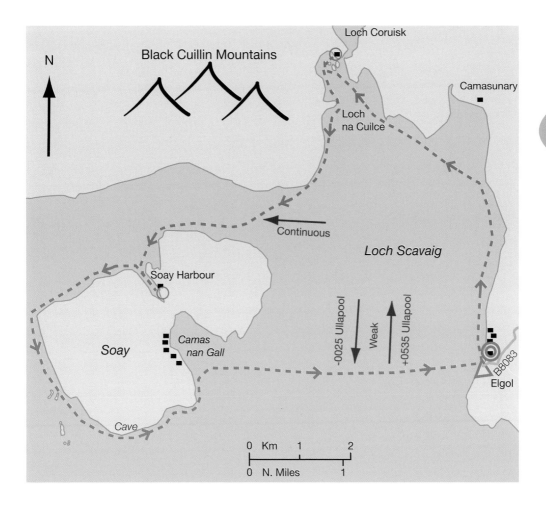

Loch Coruisk and Soay

Basking Sharks

These sharks come into Scottish waters every summer and are sometimes seen at quite close quarters by sea kayakers in calm weather. They are the second largest sharks in the world, measuring up to 12m long. They are also one of the least-known sharks, with many habits that are unexplained. They are usually spotted on their own, but it is possible to see them in groups as large as fifteen in number, cruising slowly at the surface of the water. Due to this habit they have sometimes also been referred to as 'sun-fish'. Whilst cruising they may well have their cavernous mouths open filter feeding on plankton, being able to filter 2000 tons of water an hour. When they are feeding you will probably see three parts of the shark protruding from the water, the nose, the dorsal fin and the tail, and each appears to move independently of the other in a snake-like fashion, so initially you might think there is more than one shark. The triangular dorsal fin often droops over with age so this can aid identification from a distance. Being a filter feeder, these sharks do not sport large teeth so they are not quite the 'Jaws' of the shark world and pose little threat to kayakers, though if you were to bash into one at speed it might thrash about a bit! The basking shark is usually greyish brown in colour, although it sometimes can also be blacker, and it has large gill slits almost encircling its head. It is believed that they live up to 40 years. They are only seen in the summer months; it is not yet clear where they go in the winter.

Basking sharks used to be hunted in Scottish waters for their oil which was taken from their huge livers that can be as much as one quarter of the total body weight.

An interesting book to read about basking sharks is Gavin Maxwell's 'Harpoon at a Venture', which describes one of the most famous basking shark fisheries in Scotland. For a more technical read, 'The Basking Shark in Scotland' by Denis Fairfax is worth hunting out.

pass the 'solar telephone exchange', which was the first of its type in the world and powers nine telephones.

After some exploration, leave Soay Harbour and continue the journey on around the island. On reaching the west coast of the island you will be rewarded with fine views out to the 'Small Isles' of Canna, Rum and Eigg. On a calm day they will look deceptively close and try to lure you out to them. The island will continue to provide interest with its wildlife and its small yet ornately shaped sandstone cliffs. Around the southern tip look out for a small cave as well as a 'saltire' in the cliffs formed by two diagonal intrusions into the parent rock. On reaching Camas nan Gall it will be time to leave Soay and embark on the final crossing back to Elgol, to finish a great day out.

Tide & Weather

This area generally offers reasonable shelter in mixed weather conditions. There can often be extreme downdrafts and winds rushing down from the Cuillin Mountains, these affecting Soay Sound the most. The west coast of Soay is also exposed to any westerly swell, which breaks over the numerous small reefs and rocks.

With the tides being generally weak in this area, timings do not unduly matter. If the benefit of any slight tidal movement is desired, then leave Elgol with the ingoing stream, which starts at about 5 hours and 35 minutes after HW Ullapool. By visiting Loch Coruisk first it also gives the benefit of the continuous west-flowing tidal stream in Soay Sound.

Soay cliff

Additional Information

There is ample parking, toilets and a post office in Elgol. There is also a telephone on Soay. There are regular seal watching boats in this area as well, so try to disturb the seals as little as possible. Gavin Maxwell's book 'Harpoon at a Venture' gives further insight into the shark fishing of the west coast of Scotland.

Wiay Island

No. 14 | **Grade B** | **18km** | **4-5 Hours** | **OS Sheet 23** | **Tidal Port Ullapool**

Start	△ Harlosh (285414)
Finish	◎ Harlosh (285414)
HW/LW	HW/LW in Loch Bracadale is about 50 minutes before Ullapool.
Tidal times	The tidal streams are unnoticeable in the loch.
Tidal rates	In Loch Bracadale the tidal rates are very weak.
Coastguard	Stornoway, tel:01851 702013, VHF Weather 0710 UT

Introduction

What Loch Bracadale lacks in tidal streams it more than makes up for in scenery. With the Cuillins on one side and Macleod's Tables on the other, Skye's most famous mountains overlook you. Add to this the spectacular cliffs and caves of Wiay and this is a great day out.

Description

The pebble beach at Camas Ban, Harlosh, where there is a fish farm makes an ideal starting point to explore Loch Bracadale. A gentle paddle will soon take you away from the houses and

on to Harlosh Point, where an immaculate sandy beach is seen across on Harlosh Island. While crossing to the island keep a watchful eye out for an eagle, which is sometimes seen in this area. On leaving the beach the east coast of the island provides ragged cliffs and a clear view on to Wiay. From the south-eastern tip of Harlosh a 2km crossing will take you into Camas na Cille on Wiay. This translates into 'Church Bay' and is the only easy landing spot on the island, other than the odd smaller pebble beach on the west. There is no longer any trace of the church that used to be on Wiay; all that can be seen nowadays are the ruins of some houses. The island never housed a great community and it was deserted in 1890 with no inhabitants since, other than the wealth of seabirds that make it their home today.

Leaving Camas na Cille head south to Rubha Garbh and it is here that the journey will take on a different feel. The cliffs will gradually steepen, overhang in places, and the sea will become more exposed to the ocean's weather. From this southern end of the island the sea stacks of Macleod's Maidens can be seen over to your right as they emerge from behind Idrigill Point. As you paddle round into Geodha nan Faochag the rock architecture will become increasingly spectacular. There are numerous small inlets, caves and a natural arch to explore, if the sea is calm enough to allow this. Hopefully it will, because as you pass under the tallest, slightly overhanging cliffs of the island at 59m, you will come across the largest cave of them all. This is a cave to house a family of giants, and upon entering you will feel very insignificant in its dark depths. For this cave alone it is worth waiting for a calm day to paddle around Wiay. On emerging from the cave, Wiay still has a few surprises, with more cliffs and a small natural arch leading on to the north of the island. Take the time to explore another couple of caves (a head torch may be useful as they go in a long way) before continuing to Tarner Island. A rocky bay on the south-eastern tip gives a good landing spot, with excellent views of the Cuillin Mountains while you have a rest. On leaving the bay it is possible to continue on around the island, keeping an ever-watchful eye out for wildlife as whales, porpoises and seals have been seen in Loch Bracadale on many occasions. Soon you will be paddling back across to Harlosh Point and into the sheltered waters of Camas Ban where the journey ends.

Tide & Weather

There are no noticeable tidal streams within Loch Bracadale, so tidal planning is not required. The loch is very exposed to any wind and swell that comes from the south and west, so reasonable weather conditions are best to make the trip as enjoyable as possible. Off the south of Wiay the sea state can often be considerably rougher than the rest of the trip, so to go into the caves the calmer the conditions the better.

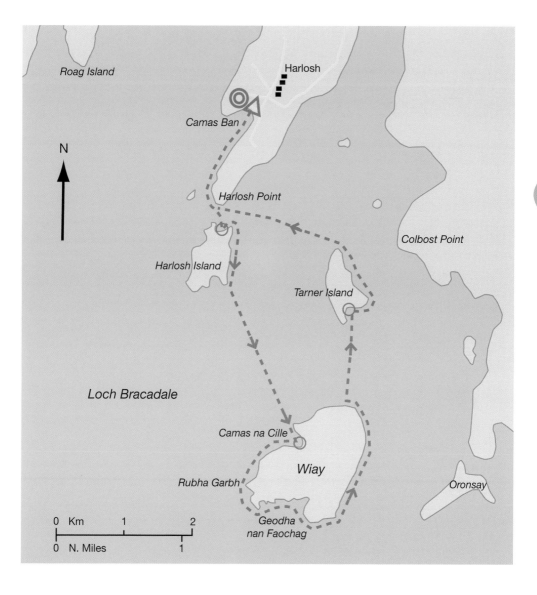

14

Caught in a Gale

It came out of nowhere, from a manageable Force 6 to an uncontrollable Force 8. The VHF came alive with other sea vessels in the area caught out and calling for assistance. I looked around at my group of eight paddlers, three were already in the water and needed rescuing. As soon as I put them back in their kayaks they would capsize again. 'Raft up to the nearest person', was all I could scream. Spray was in my eyes and the situation was out of my hands, but at least the group was upright in three small rafts in amongst the frenzied seascape. Would we be smashed on the cliffs of Harlosh Island or be blown into the sheltered beach in its lee? Soon we were huddled in a group on the beach sipping a warm drink with hands still shaking with adrenalin. The wind had died a bit and it would be possible to make it back to the bus. Good planning meant we had not been anywhere far away from land, but what if we had not thought and had been blown offshore?

Neist Point

No. 15 | Grade C | 32km | 8 Hours | OS Sheet 23 | Tidal Port Ullapool

Start	△ Meanish Pier in Loch Pooltiel (155505)
Finish	◎ Camas Ban in Loch Bracadale (284413)
HW/LW	HW/LW in Loch Dunvegan is about 45 minutes before Ullapool.
Tidal times	Off Neist Point: The N going stream runs between 4 hrs 15 mins before and 2 hrs 10 mins after HW Ullapool. The SE going eddy in Moonen Bay starts about 35 mins before and continues until about 2 hrs 10 mins after HW Ullapool. The S going stream runs between 2 hrs and 10 mins after and 4 hrs 5 mins before HW Ullapool. The NW going eddy in Moonen Bay starts about 5 hrs and 35 mins after and continues until about 4 hrs and 5 mins before HW Ullapool. Between Neist Point and Loch Bracadale: The NW going stream starts around 5 hrs and 25 mins after HW Ullapool. The SW going stream starts around 35 mins before HW Ullapool.
Tidal rates	Neist point is a very active piece of water; try your best to be here when the streams are changing direction.
Coastguard	Stornoway, tel:01851 702013, VHF Weather 0710 UT

Introduction

This is another relatively committing journey. There are few landing spots and even if you could land it would be a long walk to any road or habitation.

The attraction therefore is the remoteness and the commitment required to kayak along a stunning section of Skye's wonderful coastline. There are waterfalls, caves, arches and sea stacks dotted along this impressive coast which forces the water into a frenzy as it passes Neist Point.

Description

Meanish Pier makes a good start for this journey, as it is only 6km from Neist Point so it is easier to time your arrival at the point to coincide with quiet waters. Travelling round in the last hour of the north-going stream shouldn't be that difficult.

A few hundred metres before the lighthouse at Neist Point is an impressive rock buttress known as An t-Aigeach (the stallion). Rock climbers have many climbs in this area to choose from, but the most impressive takes a line directly up this buttress to the highest point. It is an extremely severe climb that is climbed in four sections, with a total length of 110m.

Once round the point, land at the jetty for a rest at least as the next landing place is almost 9km away at Lorgill Bay. The lighthouse was manned until 1989 when it was automated and the associated living quarters can now be let for holidays.

Moonen Bay by its very shape would suggest that it has been created by eddies that run around its shores. This bay was where Gavin Maxwell and his crew often came across basking sharks.

Gavin Maxwell, author of 'Ring Of Bright Water', a well-known book about otters, had a factory on the island of Soay, which is 45km to the SE from Neist Point. The factory processed basking sharks, which Gavin used to hunt and catch by harpoon, towing the carcass back to Soay. His book 'Harpoon at a Venture' is well worth a read for an insight into shark fishing in this area after the Second World War.

Lorgill Bay, where a landing should be possible, is a welcome break especially if you didn't stop at Neist Point. The people that used to croft this land back in 1830 were one day given an ultimatum when the landlord decided that he wanted to clear the land. It was to get on a boat and be shipped elsewhere or go to prison. Lorgill Bay is worth considering as a place to stop overnight if you want to make this into a 2-day trip.

The next section of coast is full of interest with caves, arches and a number of waterfalls that are reminiscent of the south coast of Mull along from the Carsaig Arches.

MacLeod's Maidens, just before Idrigill Point, are sea stacks named in memory of three female members of the MacLeod family who drowned at sea many years ago.

Turning north round Idrigill Point into Loch Bracadale opens up a new view with Wiay Island at its entrance, with Harlosh and Tarner islands to the left and the Cuillins of Skye in the background. If you need a break before landfall at Camas Ban, you might get ashore at Camas na h-Uamha (cave bay).

If you haven't been to Harlosh Island before it is worth stopping here on the way. It has a wonderful sheltered sandy beach on its north side.

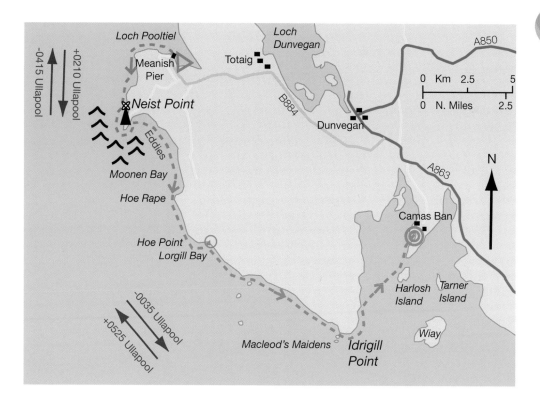

Tide & Weather

Ideally, to do the trip as described a very light wind from the NE is best, with no swell coming in from the SW. If a strong NE wind is blowing, apart from the fight back to Camas Ban from Idrigill Point, there could be some severe gusts and downdraughts from the high cliffs between Neist and Idrigill.

When the north-going stream runs past Neist Point at springs, it creates a rip, which extends for about 3km to the NW of the point.

Leaving Meanish Pier about 40 minutes after HW Ullapool should mean you arrive at Neist Point close to the end of the last hour of the north-going stream.

Additional Information

Doing this trip the other way round might indeed give you better photo opportunities as the sun will be more behind you or coming in from your left, but the big factor in deciding which way round to do this trip will be where the wind is coming from.

The roads are relatively quiet in this area and hitching back for your car might take some time. Consider calling for a Dunvegan taxi.

Dunvegan Castle

Dunvegan to Stein

No. 16 | **Grade A** | **16km** | **4-5 Hours** | **OS Sheet 23** | **Tidal Port Ullapool**

Start	△ Dunvegan (245497)
Finish	◎ Stein (264564)
HW/LW	HW/LW in Loch Dunvegan is around 45 minutes before Ullapool.
Tidal times	In the loch the direction and the times of the small amount of tidal flow is variable.
Tidal rates	The tidal streams in the loch are very weak. The maximum spring rate may be found in the channel south of Isay and will not exceed 0.5 knots.
Coastguard	Stornoway, tel:01851 702013, VHF Weather 0710 UT

Introduction

This trip offers wildlife, history, geology, coral beaches and a pub to finish. On a hot summer's day, it is fantastic to linger and enjoy the unique coral beach. On a day with strong winds, the area still offers shelter to enjoy a paddle when most other venues are too exposed. Loch Dunvegan offers a sea kayaker incredible diversity and a great day in any conditions.

The head of Loch Dunvegan and the Cuillin Mountains

16

Dunvegan to Stein

Description

Setting off from the small seaweed-covered beach you are instantly surrounded by the wildlife haven of Gairbh Eilein. As well as a variety of bird life you will be paddling amongst the resident common seals. Enjoy your ringside seat, but try not to disturb them as there are regular seal-watching boat trips in this area. If you have time you may want to continue exploring the wildlife by paddling across to Eilean Dubh before heading northwards up the loch. Camalaig Bay gives a stony beach to land on, and also gives the opportunity to explore the remains of a broch on the hillside above. Heading up the coast towards the island of Lampay you will have ever-improving views of the majestic Outer Hebrides. On a clear day you can see the islands of North Uist, Harris and Lewis. When arriving at Lampay you will see the beautiful coral beach opposite, which is an ideal place to land. The fantastically ornate pieces of white 'coral' that make up this beach are technically 'algae', but 'algae beach' has not quite the same appeal!

Leaving the beach make the small crossing to the island of Isay, the Norse name translating into 'Porpoise Island'. This is no coincidence and I have had some of my best sightings of porpoises in this area, as well as otters, eagles and a host of bird life. It is well worth paddling around the west side of Isay and exploring the islands of Mingay and Clett. These islands give continued wildlife along with some good examples of basalt cliffs. Whilst coming down the east side of Mingay you will also notice the small disused lime kiln, which is unique in its setting. Before leaving the islands take the time to land at the old abandoned village on Isay's eastern shore. In the 1800's this island supported a community of 90 people, with its own fishing station and general store. Today you can explore the ruins of over eighteen cottages and black houses, along with the grand main house. This main house was the scene of a gruesome massacre in the 16th Century, when Roderick MacLeod owned it. He wished his grandson to inherit the island, but unfortunately there were two families with first claim to the island. To solve this inheritance problem he invited them all to a big meal, and after eating called the potential inheritors of the island into his room for discussion. As each inheritor came for their discussion with MacLoed they were duly murdered until his grandson was left as the sole inheritor of the island.

Having taken in the unique natural and human history of Isay, then the picturesque village of Stein is the finishing point. On route there it is well worth passing the small skerry of Sgeir nam

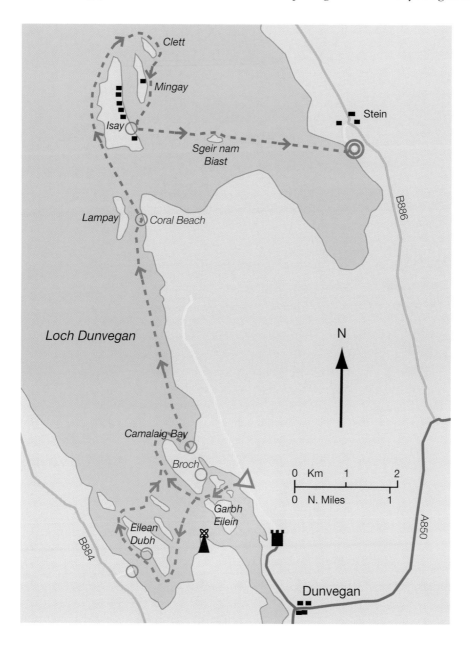

Porpoise

16

Porpoises

Whales, dolphins and porpoises are collectively known as cetaceans, and the harbour porpoise is the commonest cetacean in British waters. They are often seen all around the Scottish coastline, but most regularly in the shallower seas around the outer isles. Of the porpoise family it is only the harbour porpoise that is normally found in the UK. They are the smallest of the cetaceans you are likely to see, growing between 1.4 and 1.9m in length. They are grey in colour with a small body and dorsal fin; it is often the fin that is seen briefly sticking out of the water that catches your eye and alerts you that there are porpoises about. When seen the porpoises will generally be in groups of between two and five, although large groups up to twelve in number are not uncommon. Unlike dolphins, porpoises are not acrobatic and will be seen calmly swimming around. The harbour porpoise rarely lives longer than eight years. They communicate by listening to and interpreting the echoes of the clicking sound they make, which if lucky you will hear when close up.

Biast for a final paddle amongst the common seals. On a sunny day you will then be able to sit in the pub garden at Stein and enjoy the sun setting over the Western Isles whilst reflecting on a great day's paddle.

Leaving Stein looking towards Isay, Mingay and Clett

Tide & Weather

This trip can be undertaken at any state of the tide, as the tidal streams within the loch are barely noticeable. The main consideration for this trip is the weather. The route described works best with the wind from a southerly direction; if it is from the north consider starting at Stein. In stronger winds the area around Isay is more exposed to the conditions and it may be worth considering just paddling out of Dunvegan and remaining in the shelter of the small islands and skerries at its southern end. Here it is protected from the full force of the sea and wind, so it is possible to paddle here when most other areas will be too rough.

Additional Information

Both at Stein and Dunvegan there are good amenities with pubs, hotels and restaurants. If a transport shuttle is not possible with two cars, consider hiring a taxi from Dunvegan to collect you at the pub in Stein. Alternatively, take 2 days to explore this area more thoroughly, one exploring the islands from Stein and the other exploring the islands closer to Dunvegan.

Dunvegan to Stein

Dunvegan to Stein

'Coral' beach

Fladda-chùain

No. 17 | **Grade C** | **25km** | **6 Hours** | **OS Sheet 23** | **Tidal Port Ullapool**

Start	△ Camas Mor (370706)
Finish	◎ Port Gobhlaig (436752)
HW/LW	HW/LW at Camas Mor is around 30 minutes before Ullapool.
Tidal times	Off Ru Bornesketaig: The NE going stream starts about 4 hrs and 15 mins before HW Ullapool. The SW going stream starts about 2 hrs and 10 mins after HW Ullapool. Off Fladda-chùain: The E going stream starts about 4 hrs before HW Ullapool. The W going stream starts about 1 hr and 55 mins after HW Ullapool. Between Eilean Trodday and Rubha na h-Aiseig: The E going stream starts about 4 hrs before HW Ullapool. The W going stream starts about 2 hrs and 25 mins after HW Ullapool.
Tidal rates	There are three areas on this trip where the tidal streams run fastest: Off Ru Bornesketaig the average spring rate can reach 2.5 knots. Off Fladda-chùain the average spring rate can reach 3 knots. Between Eilean Trodday and Rubha na h-Aiseig the average spring rate can reach 2.5 knots.
Coastguard	Stornoway, tel: 01851 702013, VHF Weather 0710 UT

Introduction

This is a big day out, which from start to finish will have you paddling in potentially strong tidal streams. When combined with open water crossings that involve being up to 6km offshore and exposed to anything the weather may throw at you, it should be clear that this is a trip not to be underestimated. In ideal conditions with good tidal planning it is an incredible environment to paddle in, amongst some of the best scenery in Scotland.

Description

Starting from the slipway at Camas Mor you will be looking straight out over the first 10km of paddling to Fladda-chùain. To get there, head first to the small basalt cliffs of Ru Bornesketaig, before crossing to our first small islands of the day. These are the rocky skerries around An t-Iasgair, which translates into 'fisherman's rock'. There is no landing place on these islands, so the basalt cliffs and grass summit stay the domain of the seabirds. In the spring there will be puffins, guillemots, razorbills and kittiwakes all nesting on this small cluster of rocks. The next 5km crosses the open sea to the islands around Fladda-chùain. During the rest of the day until reaching Eilean Trodday you are paddling through one of the main shipping lanes of the Minch, so keep a watchful eye over your shoulder.

The first island of this group that you will come across is Lord Macdonald's Table, which at the right tidal level has a fantastic cave that can be paddled through to reach the other side of the island. Having paddled through this you will pass the basalt columns of the Cleats, before heading around Gaeilavore Island and on to Fladda-chùain. This is the largest of the islands and offers an easy landing place, a small natural inlet found on the south-western side of the island midway up. The island has been lived on in the past and the only evidence of this today is the ruin of a chapel. This is believed have been founded in Columba's time, and built by a huge monk known as O'Gorgon. All you will find living on the island these days is a mass of bird life, as well as giant black rabbits! The views across to the Shiant Isles and Outer Hebrides on one side, on to Cape Wrath in the other direction and the north of Skye in front, are just stunning. All this and surrounded by wildlife, history and tidal races makes this a very special island to visit.

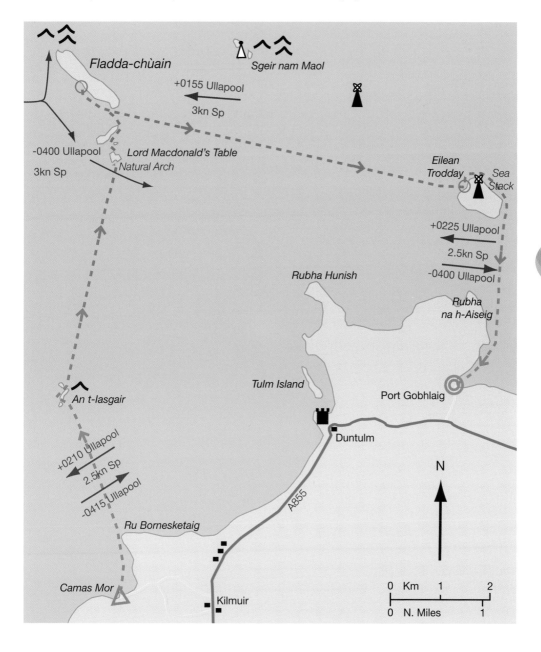

Fladda-chùain

For the next 7km you will now be on the open sea, passing the skerries and tidal race off Sgeir nam Maol on the left and the imposing cliffs of Rubha Hunish on your right, heading for Eilean Trodday. On arriving at Eilean Trodday you will have been guided there by its lighthouse, one of the smallest in Britain. There is a possible landing place on its north-western side, but it is not easy, so to continue the trip to the finish may be a better option. If you do manage to land, you may find the remains of the settlement and chapel this island used to support. Nowadays your only company will be the sheep that are put on the island for grazing. Paddling round Eilean Trodday on the north side is well worth it for the basalt cliffs and the sea stack of Bodha Trodday, before heading to the finish at Port Gobhlaig. This gives a natural sheltered bay to finish the trip, with plenty of parking for vehicles. On returning by road to the start, you will be able to see the islands that you were looking out from not so long ago.

Tide & Weather

The weather needs to be just right for this trip to be possible, and for that reason, when that settled spell of light winds arrives the journey seems that much more special. Assuming light winds then it is the tidal planning that is the main consideration for this trip. It is possible to have assistance from the tide on the entire route, and this makes the paddling far easier.

Leaving Camas Mor at the start of the NE going stream works best, about 4 hours and 15 minutes before HW Ullapool. This allows the crossing of the tidal stream to An t-Iasgair to be done in the first hour, when the use of a transit will allow an easy crossing. From here the tide will assist you on to Fladda-chùain, however on the final kilometre the tidal stream will be pushing to the south-east. With this in mind head to the western side of the islands and use a transit for the

Lunch break on Fladda-chùain

Submarine Alert

I looked over my shoulder to take in the spectacular view back towards Skye and from out of nowhere it appeared. A huge black object, powering through the seascape faster than any boat would normally travel. My heart jumped and the hairs on the back of my neck were standing tall. All of a sudden I felt very small out on the ocean, amongst tidal races and islands off the northern-most point of Skye. I had only about 500m to go until I would reach the islands of Fladda-chùain and sanctuary from the black monster getting closer all the time. I arrived at the islands and while catching my breath I watched with awe as the huge nuclear submarine powered past. Had I been a little slower, I suspect I wouldn't have made much of a dent on its nose!

final section, to reach Lord Macdonald's Table easily. It will be in the third and fourth hour of the tide when you leave Fladda-chùain, and this will give rise to the tidal race off the north-western corner of the island. This considered it might be easier to leave via the south-east end of the island and use the main push of the tide to take you on to Eilean Trodday. The tide will work well for you here, but be careful not to drift too far to the north. The tide will be dying down for the final paddle across the tidal stream between Trodday and the mainland, and it will be easy to maintain a transit.

Group landing on Fladda-chùain

If the tidal times make the trip impossible in this direction, then leaving Port Gobhlaig at the start of the west stream, 2 hours and 25 minutes after HW Ullapool, is another possibility.

Additional Information

Watch out for shipping and submarines in this area, as both regularly use it.

Rubha Hunish

No. 18 | **Grade C** | **20km** | **5-6 Hours** | **OS Sheet 23** | **Tidal Port Ullapool**

Start	△ Staffin Slipway (495683) or at smaller slipway (491686)
Finish	◎ Duntulm (408736)
HW/LW	HW/LW at Duntulm is around 30 minutes before Ullapool.
Tidal times	Off Rubha Hunish: The SW going stream starts about 2 hrs and 10 mins after HW Ullapool. The NE going stream starts about 4 hrs and 30 mins before HW Ullapool. Off Rubha na h-Aiseig: The W going stream starts about 2 hrs and 25 mins after HW Ullapool. The E going stream starts at about 4 hrs before HW Ullapool. Off Staffin Island: The N going stream starts at about 1 hr and 15 mins before HW Ullapool. The S going stream starts at about 4 hrs and 40 mins after HW Ullapool.
Tidal rates	There are two areas on this trip where the tidal streams run fastest: Off Rubha Hunish the average spring rate can reach 3 knots. Off Rubha na h-Aiseig the average spring rate can reach 2.5 knots.
Coastguard	Stornoway, tel: 01851 702013, VHF Weather 0710 UT

Introduction

This trip involves one of the classic headlands of Scotland. It has everything you would expect from such a trip including exposed coastlines, majestic cliffs, tidal races, caves and arches. Whilst paddling around this northern tip of Skye you will see the Western Isles to one side and the mainland coastline stretching to Cape Wrath on the other. With Rubha Hunish being a good place to see whales as well, it is a journey guaranteed to excite.

Description

Set off from either the pier at Staffin, or shortly before it at the small sandy beach below the corner of the road at An Corran, where a concrete ramp leads down to the beach. Then make the small crossing to Staffin Island. This island is the home of many nesting gulls, oystercatchers and curlews, which will surround you as you paddle past. From here head to Eilean Flodigarry and the impressive basalt cliff that guards its southern end. Passing under the cliff, watch out for the reefs as you pass between it and Sgeir na Eireann. This area of sheltered water is the home of many common seals that will come out to play as you paddle past. There is no simple landing here due to seaweed-covered rocks, however it is as easy a landing place as you are going to find for a while so a stop is recommended if possible. On leaving Sgeir na Eireann head across to the cliffs at Creag na h-Eiginn. For the next 4km the basalt rock architecture is quite stunning, and there are caves and arches hidden around every corner. Shortly after you start paddling along the cliffs, opposite Clach nan Ramh you will pass under Flodigarry Cliffs, which is a popular climbing venue. Here there is a fantastic cave with many through routes and tunnels depending on the tide. There will be plenty more caves to explore as you continue, but ensure that you do not miss the dramatic arch and caves in the area by Stac Buidhe. As you cross Kilmaluag Bay you will see to your left Port Gobhlaig, which gives an alternative starting or finishing point. There is a rocky beach on the north side of this bay providing a convenient landing site; it also has the remains of an old fishing station.

Having rested and eaten it is now time to head on to the climax of our journey, paddling round the northern tip of Skye. You will soon pass Rubha na h-Aiseig where the first of the tidal streams will be noticed squeezing between this headland and Eilean Trodday. At the same time the view will open out; from right to left you will see the mainland of Scotland with Cape Wrath in the far distance, the Shiant Islands to the north with Lewis to the right and Harris to the left

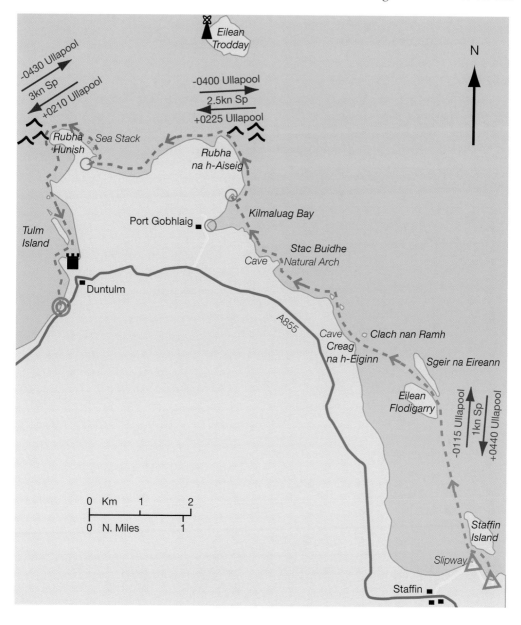

behind. The sea will most probably start to come alive, as this section of coastline is exposed to all weathers. Above there will be gannets circling and diving and below you may be lucky enough to see a minke whale. You can stay out from the cliffs and gain the most assistance from the tidal stream, but I would recommend exploring the coastline, as there are still a few more hidden caves and stacks. Just before going around the Rubha Hunish headland there is a possible rocky landing place at the western end of the bay if a rest is needed. Follow the basalt cliffs round to Rubha

Kittiwakes

Of all the gulls that grace our cliffs the kittiwake must be the most attractive. It is of a more delicate frame with a beautiful clean white and light grey plumage and a call that is so distinct it gave the bird its name. In fact a cliff without the call of kittiwakes is a dull place in comparison. Nesting kittiwakes gather together bits of vegetation and then cement it all together with droppings to make a robust nest on the smallest of ledges; indeed the nest often overhangs the ledge. Below the nest the steep cliff has the kittiwake's signature painted all over it, a splash of whitewash which often contrasts greatly with the darker rocks of the cliff. In years gone by the feathers of this beautiful bird were sought after to grace ladies' hats. The numbers of kittiwakes have increased since they were given protection from people who used to shoot them for sport and those who killed them for their fine feathers. On many of the trips in this book where there are steep cliffs, kittiwakes will be found nesting.

Kittiwakes and chicks on nest

Hunish, where there are two final sea stacks to weave in and out of. The tide will take you around the headland and lead you into the bays on the western side. If there is any wind and swell from the west this will provide some rougher conditions, but the bays can offer shelter. Continue down the coast past Tulm Island, choosing the dramatic west side or the sheltered east. Again the island is covered with bird life, and otters have been seen on the sheltered eastern side. The imposing ruin of 15th Century Duntulm Castle guards the final small headland you will pass before reaching the finish. A rocky beach landing, sometimes a small amount of sand to land on at the northern end, will be the final challenge. If this is looking too difficult in the conditions an alternative is at Port Duntulm, but ask permission at the hotel.

Flodigarry

Tide & Weather

To complete this trip you will paddle on all aspects of coast, each being very exposed to any wind or swell. With this considered, settled weather is best for the trip. If this is not possible, a shorter trip between Staffin and Port Gobhlaig, to avoid unfavourable conditions out at Rubha Hunish, is a good option and can be paddled in either direction.

It is best to time the trip so as to make good use of the tidal stream assisting you. So it is worth timing your journey to arrive at Rubha na h-Aiseig near the start of the west-going stream, 2 hours and 25 minutes after HW Ullapool. If this is done you will have had the small amount of tidal flow, no more than 1 knot average spring rate, assisting you up the east coast, before joining the main tidal stream around the northern tip. Leaving Staffin at about HW Ullapool works well to have the tide with you all the way, ensuring you have at least 6 hours of daylight for the trip. If the tides do not work out for this, then doing the trip in reverse will most probably be possible. Timing it to be at Rubha Hunish with the start of the NE going stream, 4 hours and 30 minutes before HW Ullapool will be required. There is often rougher tidal water off the two northern headlands, with the tidal race at Rubha Hunish bigger on the NE stream.

Additional Information

In Staffin there is a shop, phone and amenities if required. There is a hotel in Duntulm. If you have the energy there is a good walk to the viewpoint overlooking Rubha Hunish, starting at the telephone box in Duntulm.

Raasay and Rona

No. 19 | Grade B | Day 1 - 29km/7-8hrs | Day 2 - 20km/5-6hrs | Day 3 - 29km/7-8hrs | OS Sheet 24 | Tidal Port Ullapool

Start	△ Sconser (525323)
Finish	◎ Sconser (525323)
HW/LW	HW/LW at Loch a Bhraige, Rona is about 10 minutes before Ullapool.
Tidal times	For Caol Mor:

The E going stream starts about 5 hrs and 50 mins after HW Ullapool.
The W going stream starts at about 10 mins before HW Ullapool.
For the east coasts of Raasay and Rona:
The N going stream starts about 55 mins before HW Ullapool.
The S going stream starts about 5 hrs and 5 mins after HW Ullapool.

In Caol Rona:
The NW going stream starts about 1 hr and 10 mins before HW Ullapool.
The SE going stream starts about 4 hrs and 50 mins after HW Ullapool.

In the Narrows of Raasay:
The S going stream starts about 5 hrs and 5 mins after HW Ullapool.
The N going stream starts about 55 minutes before HW Ullapool.

Tidal rates There are four areas on this trip where the tidal streams run at their fastest:

Campsite at Acairseid Mhor, Rona

In Caol Mor the average spring rate can reach 1-2 knots.

Off the east coast of Raasay and Rona the average spring rate can reach 1 knot.

In Caol Rona the average spring rate can reach 2 knots.

In the Narrows of Raasay the average spring rate can reach 3 knots.

Coastguard   Stornoway, tel:01851 702013, VHF Weather 0710 UT

Introduction

To paddle around the islands of Raasay and Rona is a deservedly popular journey. It offers two contrasting islands with a common theme of unrivalled wildlife and unique views across to the Quiraing of Skye. Being sheltered from the westerly winds by Skye this area often provides better weather and lighter winds in which to enjoy the journey. This trip can be done in three days, but considering its interest many would choose to take longer.

Description

Setting off from the ferry terminal at Sconser provides the quickest access across to Raasay to start the journey. After the short crossing to the southern extremity of Raasay, head through Caol Mor, passing the light at Eyre Point. This leads to the remote and inaccessible east coast of the island. This entire coastline has no road access and has steeply wooded hillsides and cliffs throughout. The uniquely shaped highest point of Raasay, Dun Caan, is prominent overhead and with luck one of the golden eagles often seen in this area may be soaring high above. Up to about

Brochel Castle the cliffs and rocks are made of sandstone offering a variety of shapes and reddish colours, with landing places available but not perfect. The road running 2km north of Brochel to Arnish is the famous 'Calum's Road'. Calum MacLeod was the postman and in the 1960's the eight families making up the Arnish community were going to leave, as they had no road access to their village. The council had refused to help so, armed with a 4 shilling book on road building Calum built his own road by hand. When he finally finished he was awarded the British Empire Medal, but he and his wife were the only remaining inhabitants. He unfortunately died shortly after in 1988. If you ever drive along Calum's road, now covered in tarmac by the council, be sure to have the tune 'Calum's Road' playing on your CD. This is a tune that can bring a tear

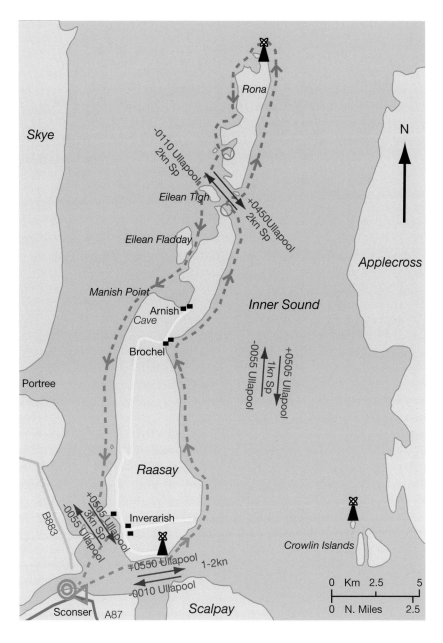

to a glass eye, knowing the effort one man went to with his bare hands, to save his community from disappearing. Leaving Brochel the island becomes more rugged and the ancient Lewisian Gneiss rock type gives the island landscape a different, rougher feel. The tiny passage between the northern tip of Raasay and Eilean Tigh provides a good sheltered stopping place. There is some camping and also the luxury of a bothy five minutes walk to the south.

Paddling across Caol Rona in the early morning sun is a magical experience, followed by continuing up the sunny east coast of Rona. With views across to the north-west highlands on one side and the remoteness of Rona on the other it is a special place. After about 3km look carefully on the hillside about 30m up for the ancient Church Cave. This is where the islanders used to worship prior to the island church being built in 1912. Although not an easy landing place it is worth the effort to explore this unique place of worship with stone pews and a natural font which receives water in the form of drips from the roof above. Further up the coast, the imposing Rona lighthouse will soon be seen as the northern tip is neared, as well as ever increasing evidence of the NATO station, which is situated here. This northern area of Rona is perhaps the most special with a mass of skerries and inlets sheltering many common seals, and otters as well. At the backs of these inlets there are often places to land and explore the area further. About 6km down the west coast of Rona, hidden behind Eilean Garbh is Acairseid Mhor, a sheltered loch that has an inlet tucked into the south-east corner. This is a fine place to camp for the second night. This natural big harbour used to be the base for the smugglers many years ago on Rona.

The final part of the journey takes you back across Caol Rona and through the sheltered Caol Fladday between the west coast of Raasay and Eilean Fladday; if it is getting towards low tide it is better to go around Eilean Fladday. Continuing down the coast the strangely shaped Quiraing

hills will be over your shoulder to the right. Also look out for the sandstone through-cave past Manish Point. With the occasional small rocky beach for a stop if required, the houses by the Narrows of Raasay will soon be reached. This will then just leave the short crossing back to Sconser to finish a fantastic journey.

Tide & Weather

The islands of Raasay and Rona generally offer relatively sheltered conditions in all but the worst of weather. Having said this, the area is still committing. There are no easy escape routes and a crossing back to Skye would only lead to a coastline with no roads.

The tidal streams produce no rough water to talk of, and generally do not affect the trip unduly. To make best use of the small tidal flow that there may be, leaving Sconser about 2 hours before HW Ullapool will take you through Caol Mor with the end of the E going stream, the W going stream starts about 10 minutes before HW Ullapool. This will then give tidal assistance up the east coast of Raasay as the north-going stream starts at about 55 minutes before HW Ullapool, and takes you to Caol Rona while it is still fairly slack. The S going stream starts about 4 hours and 50 minutes after HW Ullapool.

To go around Rona the tides have minimal effect so timings are not too important. Leaving Rona to return to Sconser to make best use of the minimal tide, leave about 3 hours after HW Ullapool, the S going stream to the west of Raasay starts about 5 hours and 5 minutes after HW Ullapool. This will get you through the Narrows of Raasay when it is relatively slack, the N going stream starts about 55 minutes before HW Ullapool.

Cave south of Manish Point

As said the tides are generally weak, so it is possible to paddle the entire trip without taking them into account. In the few areas where it flows faster, you can easily paddle against it keeping close to the shore.

Additional Information

The tune, Calum's Road can be found on the CD 'The Blood is Strong' by Capercaillie.

Whilst the owners of Rona welcome kayakers and campers they ask that we act considerately. Please do not camp within sight of houses or anywhere in the restricted area around the lighthouse at the north end. If you would like further advice please call at Rona Lodge or check www.isleofrona.com. Bothy accommodation and shower are available at Rona Lodge.

Happy landing at Crowlin Harbour

Crowlin Islands

No. 20 | Grade A | 25km | 6 Hours | OS Sheet 24 & 33 | Tidal Port Ullapool

Start	△ Kyle of Lochalsh (760276)
Finish	◎ Kyle of Lochalsh (760276)
HW/LW	HW/LW at the Crowlin Islands is about 20 minutes before Ullapool.
Tidal times	Around the Crowlin Islands: The NW going stream starts about 10 mins before HW Ullapool. The SE going stream starts about 5 hrs and 50 mins after HW Ullapool.
Tidal rates	There are two areas on this trip where the tidal streams run fastest: In Caolas Mor the average spring rate can reach 1 knot. In the Inner Sound the average spring rate can reach 0.5 knots.
Coastguard	Stornoway, tel:01851 702013, VHF Weather 0710 UT

Introduction

The tightly clustered Crowlin Islands situated off the remote Applecross peninsula provide a fine day out with their unique natural harbour and fine views across to Raasay, Rona and the Cuillins of Skye. With a short crossing to the islands and the usual common seals for company these relatively sheltered islands are worth a visit.

Dun Caan, the highest point on Raasay

Description

The Kyle of Lochalsh provides an easily accessible starting point for this trip. The launch site is in the small natural inlet, behind a football field on the west side of the town. Leaving this sheltered water and heading along the coastline towards Erbusaig Bay gives a perfect warm up for the crossing out to the Crowlin Islands that follows. Along this coastline there are numerous skerries and islands, which are owned by the National Trust for Scotland. These provide shelter for seals and otters that are regularly seen in this area. On arriving at Black Islands at the mouth of Erbusaig Bay it is time to head off on the 7km crossing to the Crowlins. Whilst enjoying the views up the Inner Sound to Raasay and Rona, as well as into the mainland mountains around Loch Carron, the crossing will pass quickly.

The first island arrived at is Eilean Mor (big island), whilst the other two, Eilean Meadhonach (middle island) and Eilean Beag (little island) will be reached shortly. Head west along the south coast of Eilean Mor to the narrow gap that separates it from Eilean Meadhonach and forms the natural harbour. It is well worth timing your arrival here to avoid low water; at this stage of the tide the entrance dries and it is not possible to kayak between the two islands. This area also provides an ideal place to have a rest after the crossing, as there is a rocky beach to land on. Leaving the beach, head through this beautiful natural harbour between the islands, which is possibly where the islands gained their name. In Gaelic Crowlin translates into 'eye of the needle channel' which as you will see is very apt. Whilst threading this needle enjoy the peace, shelter and hopefully the wildlife that this unique channel offers. Exiting the harbour on the northern side head on around Eilean Beag. Whilst paddling around this island you will be rewarded with the trip's best views up the Inner Sound to Raasay, Rona and the Applecross peninsula, along with ornate sandstone cliffs. On the western side look out for the old cable handrail, which used to help men access the light positioned higher up the steep shoreline. You will pass under the light as you paddle around the exposed northern tip of this island. Having explored Eilean Beag paddle down through Caolas Mor on the east side of the islands. Look out for numerous sea urchins, especially at low spring tides, that are readily seen around the Crowlins as you paddle down the coastline of Eilean Mor. Soon you will arrive at the last landing site on the Crowlins at Camas na h-Annait. This bay gets its name from the small church that was once situated next to it, along with the ruined cottages of the 40 islanders who used to live here in the 1840's. Having landed and had a rest, paddle on down past the final small sandstone cliffs of the Crowlin Islands until the open water back to the Kyle of Lochalsh lies ahead. From here head out on the final crossing, with hopefully a wind at the back, to return to where the journey started.

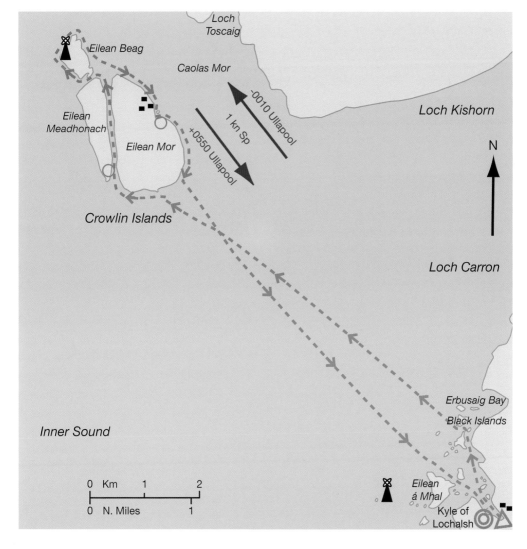

Leaving Camas na h-Annait

Tide & Weather

Generally this area provides reasonably sheltered weather conditions and as such is an ideal first open water crossing to attempt. Nonetheless, any crossing entails a certain amount of commitment, so careful weather watching is still recommended.

The tidal streams in this area are fairly negligible, so timing the trip to ensure that the natural harbour can be paddled through is of more importance. With this in mind it is best to time the arrival at the Crowlin Islands to be at high water, about 20 minutes before HW Ullapool. Leaving Kyle of Lochalsh about 2 hours and 20 minutes before HW Ullapool should facilitate this. Although this will mean that the slight tidal streams will be paddled against in order to arrive at the Crowlins at high water, it will be during the last and first couple of hours of these tidal streams. This will mean that even on a spring tide the strongest tidal streams in Caolas Mor will be no more than about 0.5 knot when they are paddled against. The rest of the trip will have less tidal movement than this.

Additional Information

There is a full range of local amenities in Kyle of Lochalsh. At the start and finish this inlet is used by local fishing boats so please park considerately.

If the gate at the put in is locked there is an alternative put in at the old ferry slipway in Kyle of Lochalsh, Grid Reference 761272. If starting here you head out using the north channel of the Skye Bridge, be aware of the small amount of tide that runs under this side of the bridge.

Sea cliffs to the west of Camas Mor

Rubha Reidh

No. 21 | **Grade B** | **18km** | **5 Hours** | **OS Sheet 19** | **Tidal Port Ullapool**

Start	△ Melvaig slip (739861)
Finish	◎ Firemore (817882)
HW/LW	HW/LW at Mellon Charles in Loch Ewe is 10 minutes before Ullapool.
Tidal times	Off Rubha Reidh:
	The NE going stream starts about 3 hrs 50 mins before HW Ullapool.
	The SW going stream starts about 2 hrs and 50 mins after HW Ullapool.
	In the entrance to Loch Ewe:
	The ingoing stream starts about 6 hrs and 5 mins before HW Ullapool.
	The outgoing stream starts about 5 mins before HW Ullapool.
Tidal rates	Off Rubha Reidh the average spring rate is 3 knots.
	In the entrance to Loch Ewe the average spring rate is 0.5 knots.
Coastguard	Stornoway, tel:01851 702013, VHF Weather 0710 UT

Introduction

This is a trip of contrasts; the first part is remote and unspoilt with a fantastic clean sandy beach where you could spend many hours relaxing. The second part is much affected by the long presence

of the Navy who used Loch Ewe as a base during the Second World War, and Loch Ewe is still a submarine exercise area with a large NATO jetty.

21

Description

Shortly after leaving Melvaig the boulder shore changes into cliffs that gradually gain in height the further north you go. There are some caves on the way up to the lighthouse. In the summer months the lighthouse is run as an outdoor centre offering walking and climbing holidays. Landing at the lighthouse is not easy, there is a little jetty beyond to the north but it would need to be quite calm before a landing could be made without hassle.

The attractive sands of Camas Mor are 2km round the corner from the lighthouse. Stopping here is a must; it is the sort of place that makes escaping from reality all the richer. Climbing up the slope behind the bay to get an overview is well worth the effort; from up here you will see Stac Bhuidhe, the yellow stack, so bright because of the orange coloured lichens growing on it. The sea will appear emerald green, contrasting with the black and red rocks of the cliffs and of course the white sands. On a fine day from here the Shiants will be visible out to the west.

The highest hill on this peninsula is Bac an Leth–choin, standing at an insignificant 284m. It was close to here that on 30th January 1878 an Arctic Fox was trapped. Arctic foxes are not native to Scotland, so this fox and others that had appeared in the same century are thought to have been brought to Scotland by whalers who had been fishing up in Greenland.

Throughout this trip there will be birds, possibly otters and porpoises, but keep a watchful eye open for white-tailed eagles (sea eagles), the largest bird in Scotland, as they have been seen before along this stretch of coast. Their wingspan can be 2.5m, so confusing them with other birds at close quarters is unlikely. If you are lucky, seeing them close up is not unheard of, they lift off from the sea cliff and fly along in front of you and perch some distance ahead, only to repeat this hopping along the coast again. A golden eagle by contrast is rarely seen so near the sea, and if you do get close to one it will more than likely fly away immediately for good.

At the entrance to Loch Ewe on Rubha nan Sasan there are the remains of a gun emplacement, a reminder of the importance of Loch Ewe as a naval base during the Second World War.

A short distance to the south is Cove, where many years ago the villagers used to worship in a sea cave. Easier to find is the natural arch on the shore close by.

By the time you reach the big sandy bay, which is split by Gaineamh Smo, the rising tide should have reduced the potentially long walk back to the car.

Tide & Weather

If the wind is blowing against the tidal stream off Rubha Reidh, heavy and dangerous seas can form, extending for many miles. A light SW wind would be preferable for this trip. A swell from the north or a strong wind from the north might make landing at Camas Mor very difficult, and this idyllic beach should not be missed. Try to arrive at the lighthouse just before the NE stream

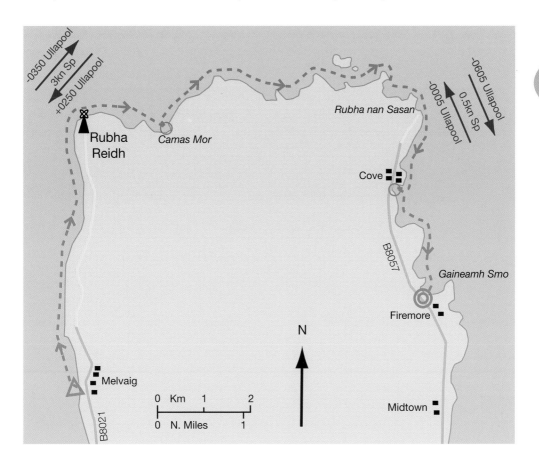

Approaching Rubha Reidh lighthouse

starts to flow, 3 hours and 50 minutes before HW Ullapool; this should ensure that you have a quiet passage round the headland. Leaving Melvaig slip about 5 hours before HW Ullapool should make the above possible.

Additional Information

To find the put-in point, follow the signs for the 'Mustn't Grumble Café Bar', a fine café that you have to pass to get on the water. There is not a lot of room for parking at the little slipway which is right outside somebody's house, so please be sensitive and consider leaving your car elsewhere if necessary.

Whilst you are in this area take a trip to the world famous Inverewe Gardens, cared for by the National Trust for Scotland, a 2,000 acre plus garden with plants and trees that many would not expect to find so far north.

Priest Island

No. 22 | Grade B | 16km | 4-5 Hours | OS Sheet 15 & 19 | Tidal Port Ullapool

Start	△ Mellon Udrigle (892958)
Finish	◎ Mellon Udrigle (892958)
HW/LW	HW/LW in the Summer Isles is about 5 minutes before Ullapool.
Tidal times	There are no noticeable tidal streams in this area.
Tidal rates	There are no noticeable tidal streams in this area.
Coastguard	Stornoway, tel:01851 702013, VHF Weather 0710 UT

Introduction

It was the naturalist Dr Fraser Darling who gave Priest Island its fame when he lived on the island in the 1930's and wrote his book, Island Years. It is no surprise that he chose Priest Island as its remote setting and lack of easy landing makes it an ideal refuge for wildlife. Add to this the caves and arches along with the idyllic sandy beach at the start and finish, and this is a great day out.

Description

The golden sand beach of Mellon Udrigle is a lovely place to start the journey, and it is also the closest point on the mainland to Priest Island. Leaving the beach and paddling along the low-lying coastline towards Greenstone Point for a kilometre soon takes you to Rubha Beag. It is from here that you are drawn by the lure of the Summer Isles to the north-east. It is about a 5km crossing to the closest of these isles, and the objective for the day, Priest Island. On the crossing the views of this fantastic part of the north-west highlands will gradually emerge. To the left will be the expanse of the Western Isles, while ahead in the foreground will be the cluster of islands making up the Summer Isles, behind lying the shapely Assynt mountains. Over your right shoulder will be the dramatic mountain of An Teallach with the island famed for being a test site for Anthrax, Gruinard Island, in the bay below.

On reaching the south coast of Priest Island, you can't but help notice the fantastically deep red colours and ornate shapes of the Torridonian sandstone that make up this island. Whilst heading east to the most sheltered landing spot on the island, Acairseid Eilean a'Chleirich, look out for the first of the natural arches and caves that litter the coastline of this island. By the time you land on the island you will have already seen a host of bird life, including eider ducks, fulmar and black-backed gulls, and it will be little surprise that the island is owned by the RSPB. With this in mind take care whilst exploring the island, as there are numerous ground-nesting birds that inhabit the island. There are small lochans, as well as remains of houses built by previous inhabitants that lived on the island long before Fraser Darling spent his time there. To the south of the most western lochan can be found a ruined bothy, which was also the site of an ancient chapel. It is this chapel that was used as a Christian retreat and is how the island acquired its name. Also in this area are the remains of prehistoric stone circles built by settlers of an even more distant past. Today you will see a shelter that the RSPB wardens use on their visits to the island.

Having explored the human history, flora and fauna, continue the island exploration by paddling up to the northern point. Here you will find Toll Eilean a Chleirich (priest hole) and on passing this you will discover the dramatic cave and natural arch making up the tip of the island. Continuing down the west coast the beautiful red cliffs create random shapes along the entire coast. Many of the seabirds use these shapes as nesting platforms, or seals pull up for a rest on them. After more geos and caves there is one final landing spot just before the most south-westerly point of the island. From here you can start your return journey back across the water to the mainland and the sandy beach finish at Mellon Udrigle.

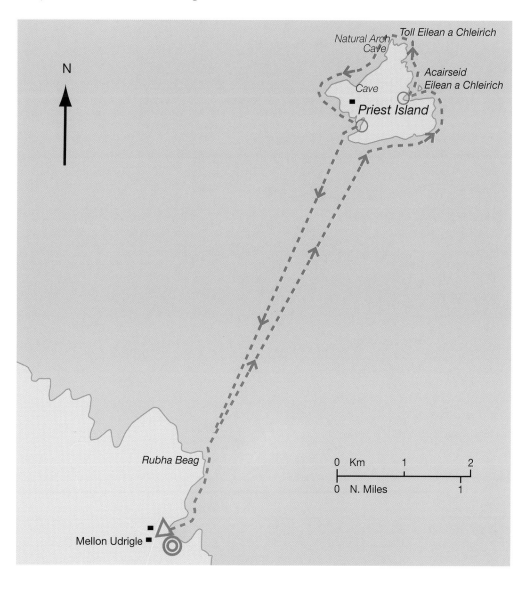

East coast of Priest Island

Tide & Weather

There are no tidal considerations for this trip, so the weather is the main concern. Priest Island has limited landing places, involves an open crossing and is exposed to potential winds and rough seas from all sides. With this considered good weather conditions are recommended for this trip.

Additional Information

There is a basic, yet fantastically situated, campsite at Mellon Udrigle. There is also a telephone box in the village, but there are no other amenities.

Cailleach Head

No. 23 | Grade B | 20km | 5 Hours | OS Sheet 19 | Tidal Port Ullapool

Start	△ Badluarach Jetty (996947)
Finish	◎ Badluarach Jetty (996947)
HW/LW	HW/LW at Badluarach is almost the same as Ullapool.
Tidal times	In the entrance to Little Loch Broom: The ingoing stream starts about 6 hrs and 5 mins before HW Ullapool. The outgoing stream starts about 5 minutes before HW Ullapool.
Tidal rates	In the entrance to Little Loch Broom the average spring rate is 1 knot.
Coastguard	Stornoway, tel:01851 702013, VHF Weather 0710 UT

Introduction

Cailleach Head translates as 'headland of the old woman'. Who the lady was or when she lived is a mystery.

For the birdwatcher this headland is an important site as it's one of the few places where all the 'divers' have been seen: great northern, red-throated, white-billed and the black-throated.

Otters are likely to be seen somewhere along this quiet coastline, especially to the east of Cailleach Head.

Description

Badluarach jetty is where the passenger ferry goes over to Scoraig, a village you can't drive to, that was repopulated in the 1960s. The village now has an almost self-sufficient community, with a primary school and a population of about 100. The village is not supplied by mains electricity from the national grid so they produce their own by harnessing energy from the wind and water, along with solar power. The community depends upon the sea and coast around the Annat peninsula for food, as the land is not the most fertile. Fish farms are a source of income for some in this area and a source of unrest for others who see the fish farms doing more harm to the environment than good.

The lighthouse is a small affair, due to the fact that the hill it stands on provides the elevation required to send the flashing light many miles out to sea. The landing jetty used to supply the lighthouse is not marked on the ordnance survey map but it is on the north coast almost a kilometre beyond the light itself. Camas na Ruthaig is an out of the way place where the chances of seeing an otter or divers is high. Carn Dearg is a heather-clad hill with some sizeable cliffs halfway up. In contrast to the generally brown hillside there are one or two rich green grassy patches, where seabirds gather.

Feith an Fheoir provides an easy place to land for a break and time to admire the view over to Ben Mor Coigach.

Further east from this bay is Achmore, even more remote than Scoraig, where a couple of families live, one of whom surprisingly provides a web design service.

The Annat peninsula has wild goats, red deer and free ranging horses, some of which you might see down close to the shore.

Journeying back you will have a good view of the Summer Isles to the north and west. Priest Island, the most southerly of the Summer Isles, was where the well-known naturalist F. Fraser Darling spent a couple of summers. His experiences are recorded in his book 'Island Years', in which you will see Fraser Darling paddling a large kayak which he used at that time.

Cross over the mouth of Little Loch Broom on the return journey to reach Stattic Point; the cliff scenery from here back to the jetty is dominated by a very richly coloured conglomerate rock that is made up of huge stones. The rock has eroded into a few narrow caves. Close by is a large fish farm which supposedly uses sound waves passed through the water to scare the seals away and therefore protecting the valuable crop of fish from predation. An unfortunate by-product of this might be that whales and dolphins also are discouraged from coming into this area.

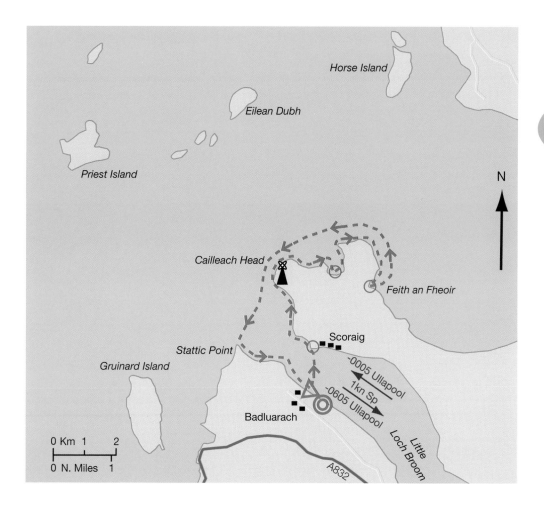

Inquisitive otter

Starfish feeding on mussels

Decisive otter

Otter

We have one type of otter in Scotland; the same animal can be seen living in fresh water and salt water environments. The otter is somewhat elusive, which is no surprise when you consider the persecution that it has suffered in the past. Otters were systematically shot and trapped as they were a threat to those with fishing interests. Prior to that, they were hunted for their fur. Otters are more active in the early hours of the morning, not long after sunrise, but it is surprising how often you can see them when out sea kayaking. They are considerably smaller than common seals, but at a distance they could be confused with a young seal. Look closer and you might see the tail at the water's surface as well as the head. Otters eat fish, shellfish, birds and if they are bold, hens and ducks on farms! Gavin Maxwell, who wrote about his basking shark fishery on the island of Soay, below Skye, also wrote a well-known book about otters, 'Ring of Bright Water'.

Tide & Weather

This is a relatively quiet bit of the Scottish coast as far as tidal streams are concerned.

With an easterly wind watch out for the funnelling effect Little Loch Broom has, the actual wind might be greater than forecast.

Conglomerate rock cliff south of Stattic Point

Additional Information

The jetty has a reasonable amount of parking, but please be careful and try to leave plenty of room close to the jetty for those going about their normal way of life.

North of Tanera Beg with Assynt mountains in background

 The Summer Isles

No. 24 | Grade A | 15km | 4-5 Hours | OS Sheet 15 | Tidal Port Ullapool

Start	△ Achiltibuie (013096)
Finish	◎ Achiltibuie (013096)
HW/LW	HW/LW at Tanera Mor is around 5 minutes before Ullapool.
Tidal times	In the vicinity of the Summer Isles the direction and times of the small amount of tidal flow is variable.
Tidal rates	The average spring rate does not exceed 0.5 knot between the islands of the Summer Isles.
Coastguard	Stornoway, tel:01851 702013, VHF Weather 0710 UT

Introduction

The area of the Summer Isles is a sea kayaker's paradise. It offers a wealth of islands, coastlines and wildlife to explore. With no real tidal concerns and relatively sheltered waters it is a perfect place to spend some time. This trip takes in the main islands on the Summer Isles, however a week could be spent fully exploring the other islands which all have a lot to offer.

125

Ornate sandstone arch on Tanera Beg

Description

Putting in at the beach to the east of Achiltibuie pier offers ample parking on the grass, looking out to Tanera Mor. A 3km crossing will take you across Badentarbat Bay to the Summer Isles, their name originating from the fact that they were used for summer grazing by the crofters. Tanera Mor is the largest and only inhabited island of the Summer Isles and its perfect large natural harbour, 'The Anchorage' is where you will first arrive. The anchorage is a very different place today to what it would have been in the late 1700's. At this time up to 200 fishing vessels would be found in the bay, bringing the herring into the fishing station at Tigh an Quay where the old pier is. Nowadays the only boats found here are usually leisure boats, and the only inhabitants on the island are there for the tourist trade. It is still worth landing to stretch the legs and explore the old schoolhouse and post office found on the island. Leaving The Anchorage head around the south of the island to Mol Mor, where you will start to get a taste for the fantastic colours and shape of the sandstone cliffs that surround these islands. Paddling around this southern side of Tanera Mor gives some spectacular views of the rest of the smaller Summer Isles, which will whet the appetite for another day's paddling.

Heading across to Tanera Beg, which has never been inhabited, it is worth paddling to the south-eastern extremity. Here you will find a beautifully ornate sandstone arch, which stands delicately over the sea. At high water it is possible to paddle a route through this arch. Leaving the arch, paddle to the sheltered lagoon found between Eilean Flada Mor and Tanera Beg, where the seals will be found lazing on the seaweed-covered rocks. At low water you will see beneath your boats, and in the small bays, coral sands that are unusual for this part of the world. There are landing spots to be found in this lagoon area if you wish to explore Tanera Beg, or spend time watching the seals.

Landing on Isle Ristol

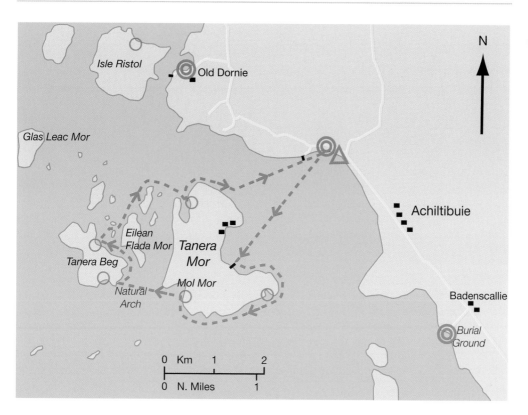

The Summer Isles

Isle Ristol

Old Dornie

Glas Leac Mor

Achiltibuie

Eilean
Flada Mor

Tanera
Mor

Tanera Beg

Mol Mor

Natural
Arch

Badenscallie

Burial
Ground

N

| 0 | Km | 1 | | 2 |
| 0 | N. Miles | | 1 | |

127

The small skerries in this area are well worth exploring for the wildlife that they hide, on your way back to Tanera Mor. The natural harbour on the north-western tip of Tanera Mor again provides shelter for the wildlife, as well as another easy landing spot before the journey back to Achiltibuie. Heading around the exposed northern tip of the island provides you with more sandstone cliffs to enjoy, along with the stunning views back to the unique north-west highland landscape. This view will guide you the final few kilometres back to the beach where you started.

Tide & Weather

With no real tidal streams in and around the Summer Isles, weather is the only consideration when planning your trip. Once amongst the islands they offer a lot of shelter from any wind or swell. Getting across Badentarbat Bay and around the exposed north and south parts of Tanera Mor require planning to make the best use of any wind and to ensure a crossing is possible there and back. If a crossing of the bay is possible but there is a rough sea off the south of Tanera Mor, then a good day's paddling can still be had using the shelter of the islands and not circumnavigating Tanera Mor.

Additional Information

Achiltibuie has good amenities including a shop, petrol station and hotel with a public bar. If you are attracted to doing further trips and explore more of the Summer Isles then there are good launching and landing sites at Old Dornie jetty (983113) and by Badenscallie burial ground (036062). If there are non-paddlers in the group there are regular boat trips to the Summer Isles in the summer season from Achiltibuie pier.

Rubha Coigeach

No. 25 | Grade B | 13km | 3-4 Hours | OS Sheet 15 | Tidal Port Ullapool

Start	△ Reiff (965143)
Finish	◎ Achnahaird Bay (016141)
HW/LW	HW/LW at Reiff is about 5 minutes before Ullapool.
Tidal times	Off Rubha Coigeach: The NE going stream starts about 2 hrs and 15 mins before HW Ullapool. The SW going stream starts about 5 hrs and 10 mins after HW Ullapool.
Tidal rates	Off Rubha Coigeach the average spring rate can reach 2.5 knots.
Coastguard	Stornoway, tel:01851 702013, VHF Weather 0710 UT

Introduction

Compared to some of the other headlands on the west coast, Rubha Coigeach is comparatively small. Some say that 'All the best things come in small packages', and this is certainly true of this journey. It has intricate sandstone cliffs, stunning views to the Hebrides and unique Assynt mountains, plenty of wildlife and a real sense of remoteness. Add to this some tidal movement and exposure to any swell or weather and it provides a great paddle.

A typical landing

Description

Starting from the sandy beach at Reiff Bay nestled below the tiny road head hamlet of Reiff, there is an immediate sense of remote tranquillity. This may soon be disturbed as the first little headland into Camas Eilean Ghlais is paddled. When there is any swell running it will be felt here, as it often kicks up over the reefs. If this proves not to your liking then head for the Summer Isles (Trip 24) for an alternative paddle. If you are happy with slightly rougher conditions then continue and enjoy. In the sheltered bay of Camas Eilean Ghlais the small but intricate sandstone cliffs can be admired, and there are likely to be seals and maybe otters enjoying the peace and quiet in this lovely bay. This is also a popular rock climbing area, so here and on up the coast there will be climbers to say hello to whilst you paddle along. As you continue up the coast, views across the Minch to the west will lead the eye to the Isle of Lewis and Harris, the mountains of Harris being due west of Rubha Coigeach. Soon you will reach Faochag Bay which has a beautifully sheltered stony beach as a landing place on its north side. This is the only easy landing spot until well round the headland so it is worth considering a stop if required.

As you round Rubha Coigeach the views are incredible. To the north is the Point of Stoer, and the Assynt mountains including the striking Suilven are to the east. The sea could well have a bit more life to it now with the tidal streams running off the point. The natural bay in the headland does not offer an easy landing, but can provide some calm water to take in the surroundings. Rounding the headland the best caves on the trip are soon discovered. There is a through route in one and a skylight in another, so be sure to look out for them. Camas Coille is next along the coastline and this provides another landing opportunity if required. Leaving here it is the final leg

Climbers on the cliffs of Camas Eilean Ghlais

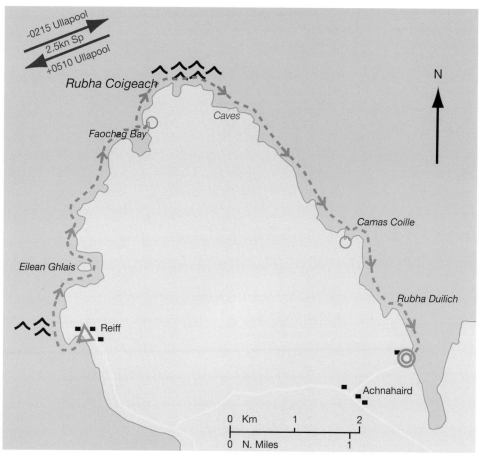

Suilven in the centre and Cul Mor to the right

of the journey to the finish at the tiny rustic slipway at Achnahaird, with the dramatic beach just beyond. Keep a watchful eye and ear open as you pass the bay by Rubha Duilich as there are often peregrine falcons nesting on the cliffs in this area. On reaching the little wooden slipway the road is a short carry away.

Tide & Weather

Rubha Coigeach does not offer many landing places and is exposed to weather and swell. With the tidal movement in addition to this, then a good weather forecast should be looked for to attempt this trip. If there are strong winds from the west then an out-and-back trip from Achnahaird is a more sheltered alternative.

It is best to paddle this route going with the flow of the NE going stream to go around Rubha Coigeach. This stream starts 2 hours and 15 minutes before HW Ullapool. The SW going stream starts 5 hours and 10 minutes after HW Ullapool, so as long as the point of Rubha Coigeach has been paddled round by this time, then the tides will be helping you throughout. On the eastern coast of the headland the tidal streams are not noticeable.

Additional Information

There is an idyllic campsite at the take-out at Achnahaird.

Off the Point of Stoer looking south

Point of Stoer

No. 26 | Grade B | 17km | 5 Hours | OS Sheet 15 | Tidal Port Ullapool

Start	△ Clashnessie (058309)
Finish	◎ Stoer (038283)
HW/LW	HW/LW at Lochinver is around 5 minutes before Ullapool.
Tidal times	Off the Point of Stoer: SW stream starts about 5 hrs 10 mins after HW Ullapool. NE stream starts about 2 hrs 15 mins before HW Ullapool.
Tidal rates	The average spring rate here can reach 2.5 knots off the Point of Stoer.
Coastguard	Stornoway, tel: 01851 702013, VHF Weather 0710 UT

Introduction

This is without a doubt one of the classic headlands of the north-west highlands, and a must for any paddler in the area. It provides the usual abundance of wildlife, spectacular cliffs and caves, limited landing spots, views to the Outer Hebrides, Stoer lighthouse and of course the 60m high Old Man of Stoer sea stack. In good conditions it provides a comfortable day's paddle, allowing time for coastal exploring or ice creams to finish.

Description

Setting out from the golden sands of Clashnessie allows easy parking and access, along with the best views of the caves and 'Old Man' while paddling around the point. The first 4km gives a gentle introduction for what is to come, with small indented cliffs and the sandy bay of Culkein (an alternative start) en route. Keep your eyes and ears alert however as there is often an otter playing in the kelp or a peregrine screeching in the cliffs along this section. As you pass Rubh'an Dunain you'll see a small natural arch up on the headland and the cliffs will start rearing up as they push towards the point. Underneath these cliffs you'll soon come to Geodha an Leth-roinn, with some narrow caves on its southern side. This offers the last possible stopping point until 6km around the point, so it may be worth the bouldery landing to rest and fuel up for a while.

The next corner to turn is the point itself and you are instantly rewarded with the expanse of the Inner Minch leading towards the Outer Hebrides. The water will start to become livelier now with the Atlantic swell and tide moving around the point. This will soon push you on a little further to get the first fantastic view of the Old Man of Stoer. As you paddle closer the grandeur of this stack becomes apparent and, in the right sea conditions, you'll be able to paddle easily between it and the mainland cliffs. Whilst doing so you may well be able to say hello to climbers scaling the stack, which was first climbed in 1966. Moving on from this be sure to save some film, as there is plenty more to come in the next 4km. These are perhaps the most impressive cliffs of our journey, along with some house-size caves, all too soon leading to the impressive Point of Stoer lighthouse.

Beyond the lighthouse the cliffs finish and the coastline changes to shingle and sand beaches. These offer a welcome landing spot for refreshment, prior to the final 5km of our journey. This takes us along a rocky coastline with some small caves at the entrance to the Bay of Stoer. Here we land on another golden sand beach with a short carry to the road, looking behind to see the sun going down over the distant Western Isles.

Tide & Weather

The south-west tidal stream of the Point of Stoer starts at about 5 hours 10 minutes after HW Ullapool. To make this journey as easy as possible it is worth timing the trip to arrive at the point whilst the tide is in this direction. The tide then starts to run in a north-easterly direction about

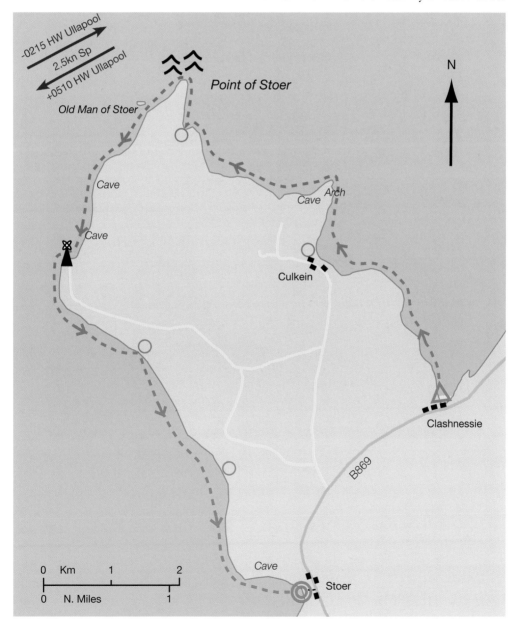

Old Man of Stoer

2 hours 15 minutes before HW Ullapool, so allow 2-3 hours from the point to reach the Bay of Stoer with the tide. Off the point on spring tides the rate will reach 2.5 knots, but this quickly subsides either side of the point. It is also possible, yet not desirable, to round the point eddy hopping against the tide at springs.

It should be noted that there are limited easy landing spots and this coastline is very exposed to any westerly winds and swell. With this in mind a good weather forecast is advised and, if the weather dictates, the route should be considered in reverse, or just going out and back to the point and stack, making use of the sheltered side of the point.

Handa Island

No. 27 | Grade B | 17km | 4-5 Hours | OS Sheet 9 | Tidal Port Ullapool

Start	△ Scourie (151446)
Finish	◎ Scourie (151446)
HW/LW	HW/LW at Scourie is around 10 minutes after Ullapool.
Tidal times	On the west coast of Handa: The SW going stream starts about 4 hrs and 30 mins after HW Ullapool. The NE going stream starts about 1 hr and 45 mins before HW Ullapool. In the Sound of Handa: The SW going stream starts about 2 hrs and 10 mins after HW Ullapool. The NE going stream starts about 4 hrs and 15 mins before HW Ullapool.
Tidal rates	There are two areas on this trip where the tidal streams run at their fastest: In the Sound of Handa the average spring rate can reach 2-3 knots. On the west side of Handa the average spring rate can reach 2-3 knots.
Coastguard	Stornoway, tel: 01851 702013, VHF Weather 0710 UT

Introduction

Handa is a nature reserve as well as a Site of Special Scientific Interest (SSSI). Both of these designations are deservedly earned and there is no better way to experience this remarkable island than by sea kayak. On a calm day the cliff architecture and cave exploration is second to none. This blended with the incredible amount of bird and marine wildlife, along with stunning views toward the Point of Stoer and Cape Wrath, make this a journey not to be missed.

Description

Starting from the sheltered golden sands at Scourie gives a perfect launching spot. It also provides an ideal place to explore the mainland Lewisean Gneiss rock cliffs, as well as circumnavigating the sandstone rock cliffs of Handa. Leaving the beach, paddle along the southern coast for a short while until Handa Island comes fully into view. At this point head across the open water aiming for the beach on the south-eastern point of the island. On the way to this beach, as well as throughout the rest of the day, keep an eye out for seals, porpoises, dolphins and whales as they can be seen in this area. Soon you will arrive at the picture-postcard beach at Port an Eilean on Handa. It is well worth stopping here, as there is nowhere else to stop on your journey on around Handa. It also gives an opportunity to take a walk on the island if time allows. Handa was used as a burial ground by the mainland settlements in early times. In those days it was quite common to bury the dead on islands as it protected the bodies from scavenging wolves, and also from evil spirits that were believed to be unable to cross open water. At its busiest in the 1840's, 65 people lived on Handa surviving off the land and sea. They operated similarly to the people of St Kilda with their own 'queen', and also with the men holding a daily parliament to decide the jobs to be done. These days if you visit in the summer months you may meet some of the five thousand visitors the island has a year, or one of the Scottish Wildlife Trust wardens who look after the island.

Leaving the beach, head along the south coast of the island to Bogha Mor where the journey will change in character quite dramatically. If there is any swell in the Atlantic it is here that it will be experienced; along with this the coastline ahead rears up to 100m sheer sandstone cliffs. If the swell allows, keeping in close to the cliffs will reveal numerous caves and arches, all guarded by the thousands of seabirds that nest on the island. Guillemots will undoubtedly make up many of these birds as Handa is the largest breeding colony of these in Britain with about 100,000 birds. In addition you will see razorbills, puffins, shag, skua and kittiwakes to name a few. With May to July being the breeding season it is worth timing your paddle around Handa to be in these months to see the island at its best. As you reach the dramatic vertical walled bay that makes up the north-western corner of the island, you may also be able to explore the sea arch that forms its northern end. Just around this on the north coast is the immense 'Great Stack of Handa', which stands 115m high balanced on three giant legs of rock. If conditions allow this is an incredible

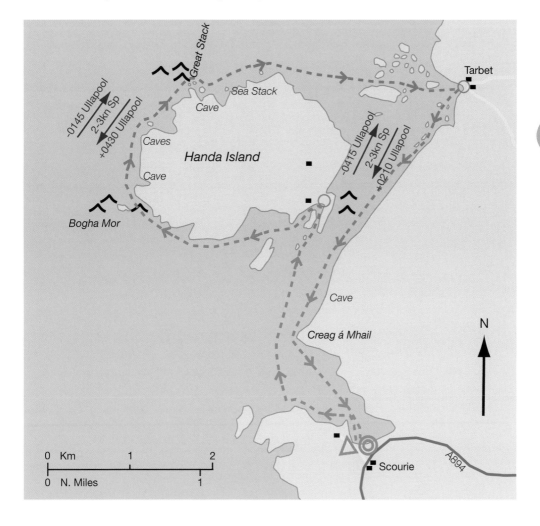

place to explore by kayak. This stack has been climbed by its north face and was first ascended in 1876 when Donald MacDonald went hand over hand across a rope attached to the mainland cliff, a brave stunt. Crossing the bay there is one more stack to explore before the cliffs slowly start to subside as the Sound of Handa is reached.

From here it is worth paddling across the entrance of the sound and through the archipelago of skerries that guard the tiny village of Tarbet. A rest can be taken here and the café may be open for an ice cream or chilled drink. Refuelled and rested, heading down through the Sound of Handa is a great way to finish the journey. The sea stack of the 'Old Man of Stoer' will be visible in the distance and on one side is a sandy beach and sandstone of Handa, whilst on the other is the shaped Lewisian Gneiss rock cliffs of the north-west highlands. These cliffs provide further interest all the way back to the beach at Scourie.

Tide & Weather

The west and north coasts of Handa are exposed to the full force of any Atlantic swell and this should never be underestimated. Add to this the numerous reefs in the area, particularly at Bogha Mor, and this can prove to be a very serious paddle in anything other than ideal weather conditions.

To make best use of the tide on this trip, time it so that the north coast is reached as the tide starts flowing in a south-westerly direction, about 4 hours and 30 minutes after HW Ullapool. This ensures that there is tidal assistance up to this point, but also that the tidal races which form off the west and north coasts are at their slackest. Leaving Scourie at about 1 hour and 30 minutes after HW Ullapool should accommodate this. When paddling through the Sound of Handa the tide will be helping, as it starts in a south-westerly direction about 2 hours and 10 minutes after

Guillemots on ledge, gannet overhead

Guillemots and Razorbills

These birds are commonly seen along the Scottish coastline, noisily crowding many of the cliffs in the nesting season. As well as the guillemot, there is also the black guillemot often but not as regularly seen. The guillemot is the most common of the auk family and is about twice the size of a puffin, grey in colour with white chest and undersides of wings. It has a longer pointed bill and flies fast and low over the water. The black guillemot is more similar in size to the puffin with a pointed beak, black in colour with white patches on the wings. When it flies it has striking, bright red, webbed feet making it easily recognisable.

Where there are guillemots there will be razorbills, yet rarely as many. These birds are a lot blacker in colour with a more striking white underside. Slightly smaller than the guillemot they have a thicker set neck and a very distinctive bill. This is shorter and thicker than the guillemot's, slightly hooked at the end with a vertical white stripe towards the front of it.

All of the above birds dive for their food, the guillemot going to an amazing depth of 180m from a sitting start. It has a reinforced ribcage to withstand the great pressures at such depths. By comparison the razorbill only manages to dive to a meagre 120m!

HW Ullapool. In the centre of the sound rough water can sometimes be experienced, particularly with a south-westerly wind against the tide.

Kayakers dwarfed by the sandstone cliffs of Handa

Using the eddies it is possible to paddle around Handa at any state of tidal stream, however on a spring tide this would be ill-advised.

Additional Information

There is a shop, campsite and local amenities at Scourie. As well as the café at Tarbet there are also toilets and a telephone box. If you wish to camp on Handa permission is needed from the Scottish Wildlife Trust, 0131 312 7765.

Barra Head

No. 28 | **Grade C** | **Day 1 - 23km/6-7hrs** | **Day 2 - 24km/6-7hrs** | **Day 3 - 12km/3hrs** | **OS Sheet 31** | **Tidal Port Ullapool**

Start	△ Castlebay, on the island of Barra (664981)
Finish	◎ Castlebay, on the island of Barra (664981)
HW/LW	HW/LW at Castlebay is about 1 hour and 10 minutes before Ullapool.
Tidal times	Between Orosay and Caragrich Island:

Between Orosay and Caragrich Island:
The E going stream starts about 5 hrs before HW Ullapool.
The W going stream starts about 1 hr and 15 mins after HW Ullapool.

In the Sound of Sandray, Pabbay & Mingulay:
The E going stream starts about 5 hrs after HW Ullapool.
The W going stream starts about 1 hr and 50 mins before HW Ullapool.

In the Sound of Berneray and off Barra Head:
The E going stream starts about 6 hrs and 5 mins before HW Ullapool, running for 4 hrs 15 mins.
The W going stream starts about 1 hr and 50 mins before HW Ullapool, running for 8 hrs 15 mins.

On the west side of the islands from Barra Head northwards:
The N going stream starts about 4 hrs and 30 mins before HW Ullapool.
The S stream starts about 1 hr and 55 mins after HW Ullapool.

Looking NE from Mingulay

On the east side of the islands from Berneray northwards:
The NE going stream starts about 5 hrs and 10 mins after HW Ullapool.
The SW going stream starts about 50 mins before HW Ullapool.

Tidal rates   Between Orosay and Caragrich Island:
The average spring rate is around 0.5 knots.

In the Sound of Sandray:
The average spring rate is around 3 knots.

In the Sound of Pabbay:
The average spring rate for the east-going stream is around 3.5 to 4 knots, and
it is strongest in the first 3 hours.
The west-going stream is weaker than the east-going stream.
Eddies form on both sides of the sound and close inshore and the streams
begin 3 hours earlier than those in the middle of the channel.

In the Sound of Mingulay:
The average spring rate for the east-going stream is around 3 knots.
The average spring rate for the west-going stream is around 2 to 2.5 knots.
Whilst the east stream is running, a heavy race extends for about 700m east
of the north point of the island of Mingulay.
Overfalls occur off the east side of Mingulay where the east-going tidal streams
from the Sounds of Mingulay and Berneray meet.

In the Sound of Berneray:
The average spring rate is around 2.5 knots.

Off Barra Head:
The average spring rate for the east-going stream is around 2 knots, the west-
going stream is less strong.

The east-going stream sets ESE off the SW coast of Berneray and NE off the SE coast where there are overfalls.

On the west side of the islands from Barra Head northwards:
The average spring rate in both directions of salient points is around 2 knots.
On the east side of the islands from Berneray northwards:
The average spring rate in both directions of salient points is around 1 to 1.5 knots.

Vatersay:
Off the west side of the northern part of Vatersay, overfalls occur.

Coastguard   Stornoway, tel:01851 702013, VHF Weather 0710 UT

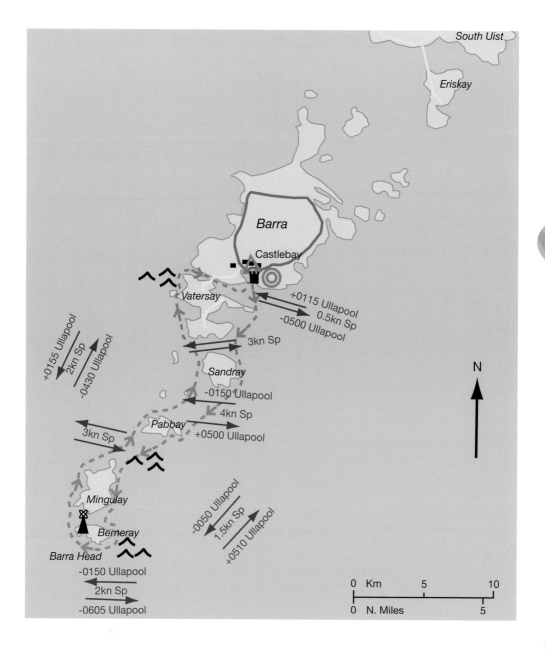

Introduction

For sheer raw beauty, immense cliffs, a feeling of solitude, feeling like an ant in a bigger world, there is nowhere like Barra Head or the south-west corner of Mingulay.

Description

The first day as described is a full day, so it is worthwhile staying in Castlebay overnight. There is no campsite, but going a short distance to the south of Ledaig (666976) should provide an acceptable wild camping spot for a night.

The island of Barra suffered from the 'Clearances' as many places in the highlands did. The people here were evicted in 1851 with the help of policemen from other places, then the homeless people were shipped off on a forced emigration, all to make way for sheep.

The most significant building in Castlebay is Kisimul Castle, a castle that is still lived in, though it was uninhabited for 200 years after it was attacked and burnt down during the late 1700's. It is the ancestral home of the MacNeils of Barra and as such attracts many MacNeils from all over the world; the castle is open to visitors at certain times during the week.

Paddling out from Castlebay has a great feeling, you know you are going on a special trip, the weather is rarely good enough for a group of kayakers to pass round Barra Head and the waiting has added to the excitement.

Before long you will have passed Vatersay and be crossing over to the sandy island, Sandray. Huge sand dunes occupy the east side of this once inhabited island. From Neolithic times until 1931 people

lived on this island, with periods no doubt when there was no one on the island as was the case in 1835 when the whole population was cleared to provide the landlord with more sheep grazing.

Pabbay is the priest's island, and the site of a chapel with a symbol stone and cross slabs is marked on the map. Bagh Ban is a lovely place to land; it has a very sheltered sandy beach that has colours good enough to grace any tourist brochure. The islanders used to fish to supplement their meagre diets, and it was whilst on a fishing trip that the island lost all of its able men to a storm in May 1887. May is usually a good time of year for the Hebrides, settled sunny weather often prevailing, but it just goes to show that even in early summer the weather can change without much warning.

Mingulay is larger than the last two islands and it supported more people, enough to warrant a school. The old village lies deserted at the back of Mingulay Bay, where you can land in preparation for staying the night. Make the time to take a walk around the island; the view from the hilltops to the other islands is fantastic, and the view from the top of the cliffs on the west coast scary! The cliffs reach an amazing height of 200m, and it is on these cliffs that many birds nest, razorbills, guillemots and kittiwakes. For the islanders, these birds provided them with a valuable food source, though at the risk of falling to their deaths trying to catch the birds or retrieve their eggs.

Berneray, the most southerly of the Outer Hebrides was last occupied in 1970 when the lighthouse keepers finally left as the lighthouse became automatic. The island does not look as though anyone other than a light keeper would live on it, but there is much evidence to suggest that man has inhabited Berneray ever since the Bronze Age. In 1881 72 people apparently eked out a living on this tiny island with no flat ground and a fickle water supply in the dry months. The cliffs below the lighthouse are 190m high but even up here, according to the keepers of the light, the sea can reach in a storm, leaving behind small fish lying in the grass at the top of the cliff.

Arch Wall, Pabbay

The west coast of Mingulay has attracted rock climbers in recent years, who scale the vertical and overhanging walls that from the sea look impossible. The rock scenery here is unique, the cliffs are on a scale rarely seen anywhere else in Scotland. Lianamul is a large stack that used to have a rope bridge across to it from Mingulay. Paddling through the gap below where the bridge used to be is awesome, how the first person got on top of Lianamul is a marvel.

Pabbay also has impressive cliffs on its west coast that are climbed. On the Arch Wall one route is described as being 'one of the finest routes in the Hebrides'; it is called 'Prophesy of Drowning'!

The bay on the NW corner of Sandray, tucked in behind Rubha Sheader provides a good place to land and camp. Prior to coming here make sure you visit the impressive natural arch on Flodday.

The journey up the west coast of Vatersay seems tame by comparison to the previous day's paddle, but nonetheless this a fine section of remote coastline. Vatersay has a causeway, which now blocks the Sound of Vatersay, but it is easy to cross, making a round trip of Vatersay within reason.

Tide & Weather

The success of this trip is dependant on a period of stable weather, where light winds are expected for the first two days at least and there is very little swell. Landing places are few and far between, and many of the normal landing spots are sandy beaches that can have a fair bit of surf if there is a swell.

Be very aware of the distance you will be from habitation and the fact that the waters down toward Barra Head are not frequented. You are very much on your own, which is most definitely one of the attractions this adventure has to offer.

Great skuas

Skuas

Despite the name, even the great skua is not a big bird, but it is a force to be reckoned with. Skuas are the pirates of the bird world; they attack other birds to steal what they have caught or just to kill the bird for a meal. We have arctic, long-tailed, pomarine as well as the great skua which is known to many as the 'bonxie'. If you are going for a walk in some of the remoter parts of the west coast, such as on the island of Mingulay whilst you are doing Trip 28, watch out for the bonxies. If you stray into their nesting territory which is on open moor / grassland these aggressive birds will attack you with vigour from the air, diving at great speed directly toward your head. It is for this reason that scientists studying skuas wear helmets to protect themselves whilst they approach nests to count eggs and later ring young chicks.

As noted above, the tidal streams run fast between the islands, and where opposing steams meet, such as they do when an eddy meets its parent flow, expect to find more turbulence. Not all eddies, overfalls and races are identified, use your seamanship to anticipate where these disturbances might occur.

Additional Information

A ferry from Oban on the mainland services Castlebay. For details of this service visit Caledonian MacBrayne's website, www.calmac.co.uk.

Passing between Lianamuil and Mingulay

If the weather is good and time permits it is worth considering extending this trip to circumnavigate Barra. From Sandray on the third day travel up the west coast of Barra and turn into the Sound of Fiaray and go across to Fuday where a camping spot can be found at the north end of Traigh na Reill. The following day return to Castlebay by kayaking down the east coast of Barra. The tidal streams in the Sound of Barra are complicated; make sure you check these out by consulting the pilot.

The beautiful sands of Ceann Ear

Monach Islands

No. 29 | Grade C | 36km | 8 Hours | OS Sheet 18 & 22 | Tidal Port Ullapool

Start	△ Hogha Gearraidh (Hougharry) Sheet 18 (705707)
Finish	◎ Hogha Gearraidh (Hougharry) Sheet 18 (705707)
HW/LW	HW/LW at the Monachs is about 1 hour before Ullapool.
Tidal times	At Aird an Runair:

At Aird an Runair:
The N going stream starts about 6 hrs before HW Ullapool.
The S going stream starts about 25 mins after HW Ullapool.

In the Sound of Monach:
The N going stream starts about 4 hrs and 30 mins before HW Ullapool.
The S going stream starts about 1 hr 55 mins after HW Ullapool.

Tidal rates
Off Aird an Runair the average spring rate is about 2 knots.

In the Sound of Monach the average spring rate is about 2 knots.

Between and around the Monach Islands where the water is shallower the average spring rate could be as much as 3 knots.

The tidal streams passing the Monach Islands are split, some of the water going to the west and some to the east of the islands, with a small amount going between. The result of this is that:
An eddy runs south toward the islands when the N stream is running.
An eddy runs north toward the islands when the S stream is running.

Coastguard   Stornoway, tel:01851 702013, VHF Weather 0710 UT

Introduction

The Monachs, a National Nature Reserve, are a group of very low-lying islands that used to be inhabited by as many as 140 people in 1891.

There is more sand than rock, beautiful shallow bays of sparkling clear water, a rich fertile machair with countless wild flowers and a fantastic view back over to North Uist.

These islands are very clearly separated by 7km of water from North Uist, but the story goes that five centuries ago there used to be a connecting bar of sand stretching all the way to Uist, that was exposed at low tide.

Today the most notable inhabitants are the ever-increasing numbers of grey seals that use the Monachs as a breeding ground at the end of each year.

Description

Hougharry sits on the northern edge of the RSPB Balranald Nature Reserve. The reserve is home to one of Europe's most endangered bird species, the corncrake, which benefits from the traditional crofting agricultural practices that are encouraged by the RSPB. The nature reserve is a beautiful mix of sandy beaches, flower-rich machair, sand dunes, marshes, shallow fresh water lochs and a rocky foreshore. During the summer months the visitor centre at Balranald is open during the day.

Once you have left Hougharry and rounded Aird an Runair, the crossing to the Monachs starts. The first place you will come to is Stockay, a favoured place for the seals. The Monachs have the largest breeding colony of grey seals in the United Kingdom producing one quarter of all the UK seal pups. If you arrive at the islands when there are seal pups try to keep disturbance to a minimum.

The seals used to be hunted by the islanders years ago and their numbers were few, but since the islands became uninhabited in 1942 when the lighthouse keepers left, the seal numbers have rocketed.

The shell sand that covers the hard bedrock makes for a fertile growing medium for the many wild flowers that add a splash of colour to the islands.

Close to the remains of the small village at the south end of Ceann Ear, areas that were cultivated can be seen. The grain from crops grown in these fields was dried in kilns that were part of the houses.

The village is now in a ruinous state, the old schoolhouse being the best preserved of all.

Monach translates to 'Monk', and it was the monks who maintained a light on Shillay to warn mariners of the group of islands a long time ago. Today the 40m high red brick lighthouse that was built in 1864 is not used.

Fulmars that would usually nest on cliffs can be found here nesting on the ground. Watch out for their oily spray if you get too close, the smell is extremely offensive. Other birds that you might see are black guillemots, terns and herons.

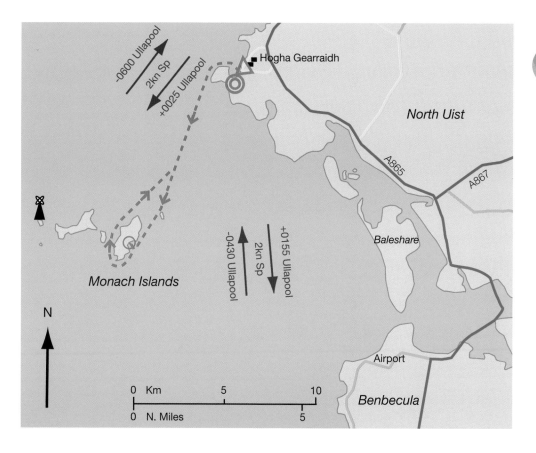

Grey seal, the hunter, dreaming of big juicy fish

Pity... it was such a nice dream!

Grey seal pup

Grey Seal

Grey seals are found all around the Scottish coastline, in particular the remoter Atlantic coastlines and islands. The UK is home to 36% of the world's grey seal population, and on the Monach Isles, off the Outer Hebrides, is the second largest breeding colony in the world. The grey seal is the largest living carnivore in Britain and is different to the common seal in a number of ways: it is noticeably bigger (average male 2.3m in length) it has a very distinctive face with a 'Roman nose' and tends to be uniform in colour (generally males are black and females are creamy white). The scientific name of these creatures means 'sea-pig with hooked nose' which neatly describes its appearance. The females have their young from the end of September to mid-December. The pups are born with a beautiful pure white coat, which used to act as camouflage when they gave birth on the ice. When born, the seals are reliant on the mother for food for up to 21 days and may stay at the breeding ground for up to another 14 days before heading out to sea. With this in mind it is important for kayakers not to disturb young grey seal pups during this period.

The traditional name of Heisker, meaning bright skerry, seems more appropriate as the shining white sands will be around forever, whereas the period when monks lived on the islands was but a brief moment in the history of these wonderful islands.

Tide & Weather

Leave Hougharry 3 hours after HW Ullapool, the south-going stream will have been running for 2½ hours now past Aird an Runair so you should be helped along nicely by the flow of water running at its fastest for the day.

It will take you 2 hours or less to reach Ceann Ear after which you can explore and relax for 4 hours at least until heading back north around the start of the north-going stream in the Sound of Monach which will be 4 hours and 30 minutes before HW Ullapool.

You will be looking for an idyllic day to do this trip, no threatening changes expected during the day. Look for a day with very little swell and a cloudless blue sky, with a light wind to stop you getting too hot.

Additional Information

Starting at Hougharry is recommended because it is sheltered and it is the closest beach to the public road. Looking at the map you will see that there are other tracks leading to the shore further south, but there would be no right of vehicular access.

Hostel on Berneray

Sound of Harris

No. 30 | **Grade B** | **29km** | **7 Hours** | **OS Sheet 18** | **Tidal Port Ullapool**

Start	△ Caolas Bhearnaraigh Slipway (907794)
Finish	◎ Caolas Bhearnaraigh Slipway (907794)
HW/LW	HW/LW in Sound of Harris is about 40 minutes before Ullapool.
Tidal times	This is a unique area for tides, which have been simplified as much as possible. There can still be variations in many areas of the sound and they are influenced by the weather so use your own observations to confirm or adapt. All the times given are for the period of British Summer Time, as they differ in winter!

Around Ensay:
At neaps the SE going stream flows all day.
At neaps the NW going stream flows all night.
At springs the SE going stream starts about 5 hrs and 35 mins after HW Ullapool.
At springs the NW going stream starts about 35 mins before HW Ullapool.

Between Berneray and Killegray:
At neaps the SE going stream lasts for 8-9 hours during the day.
At neaps the NW going stream lasts for 2-4 hours during the day.
At springs the SE going stream starts about 5 hrs and 5 mins after HW Ullapool.

At springs the NW going stream starts about 1 hour and 35 minutes before HW Ullapool.

Tidal rates There are two areas on this trip where the tidal streams run at their fastest: In the small channels around Ensay the average spring rate can reach 5 knots. Off the NE coast of Berneray the average spring rate can reach 3 knots.

Coastguard Stornoway, tel:01851 702013, VHF Weather 0710 UT

Introduction

The Sound of Harris provides one of the most interesting and unique paddling venues in Britain. The tidal streams are a law unto themselves and work differently to anywhere else you are likely to paddle. The scenery of perfect beaches, seal laden skerries, beautifully situated islands, an array of seabirds, crystal clear waters and breathtaking views make this a place to spend a lifetime exploring. This paddle will just scratch the surface of what this area can offer, but will be enough to leave any paddler wanting more.

Description

The slipway overlooking Caolas Bhearnaraigh on the northern tip of Uist is an ideal starting place to explore the sound. Leaving here head across to the east coast of Berneray, paddling the route of the new causeway that has replaced the ferry. Along the coastline of Berneray you will see the numerous original black houses in amongst the modern houses of today's community. There are also some restored black houses on the island that it is possible to stay in if desired. Looking out from the island there is just a mass of small islands and skerries in all directions out into the sound. Some of these will be explored on this trip, however the majority will be left for a lifetime of future paddling trips. Soon you will leave the houses and beaches and the coastline will turn into the ancient Lewisian Gneiss rock. Views to the north and west will start to unfold. It will be the island of Pabbay that will come into view out in the Atlantic, but keep a watchful eye on the far horizon beyond this and you may be lucky enough to get a glimpse of St Kilda nearly 50 miles away.

From the NE coast of Berneray it is time to head out across the sound for the north of Ensay. You will paddle past some skerries off the north of Killegray, hopefully seal laden, before reaching the stunning shell sand beach, Manish Strand. Stopping to enjoy this beach is well recommended as it has some history to explore as well. On one of the beach's tidal islands you will discover an old burial ground, the wall of which is thought to date back to the 9th Century. Near this a 12th Century chapel was also discovered in the 1970's, which was buried in the sands, this might also be visible. Pushing off from the white sands and entering the crystal clear turquoise water, head around the northern point, to continue the journey down the east coast. Just before another beautiful beach and the uninhabited Ensay House, there is a standing stone on the hillside, providing evidence that prehistoric man visited these islands and I am sure they were also taken by their beauty. If a brief stop is taken at the beach of Ensay House, take a look at the restored chapel just alongside it whilst you are there.

Continuing south around the mass of small skerries off the south of Killegray, you will be kept company by the wildlife. If the weather is good the views beyond these skerries to Skye and the mainland are stunning. At the southern tip of these Killegray skerries it is very tempting to just continue exploring these wildlife havens of crystal waters and if time allows this is worth doing. You could stop at one final fantastic beach, situated on the south side of Killegray, before heading back towards Berneray. Visiting the final skerries of the journey on the crossing back will provide further wildlife, and if very lucky there may even be dolphins around to keep you company. On completing the journey it will no doubt leave plenty of memories, but also plans to go back and visit further parts of the Sound of Harris.

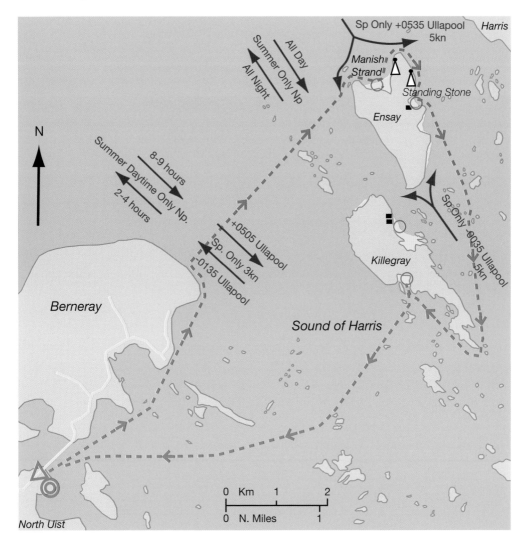

Harris and Berneray

Tide & Weather

Reasonable shelter from the weather can be found in the Sound of Harris. If it is marginal conditions for the exposed crossings out to Ensay and Killegray, then alternative sheltered trips are easily found on the south side of the sound and into Loch Maddy.

Due to the potentially complex nature of the tides in this area, it is recommended to do this trip on neap tides initially. If this is the case and the trip is done in summer, then the tidal stream will generally be running in a SE direction throughout. With this considered, whilst crossing from Berneray to Ensay ensure to work with transits so as to maintain good course. For the rest of the trip you will have tidal assistance, with the following of transits required for the crossing back to Berneray.

If doing the trip on spring tides then it is best to time it so that north of Ensay is reached at the start of the SE stream, 5 hours and 35 minutes after HW Ullapool. This will provide some tidal assistance on the crossing to Ensay, and then tidal assistance whilst paddling to Killegray. On the final crossing careful use of transits will be required to effectively reach the slacker water south of Berneray.

Additional Information

There is a post office on Berneray. Care should be taken of the ferries that regularly cross the Sound of Harris.

Taransay

No. 31 | **Grade B** | **27km** | **6 Hours** | **OS Sheets 13 & 18** | **Tidal Port Ullapool**

Start	△ Loch Leosavay (Amhuinnsuidhe) Sheet 13 (046078)
Finish	◎ Loch Leosavay (Amhuinnsuidhe) Sheet 13 (046078)
HW/LW	HW/LW on Taransay is about 55 minutes before Ullapool.
Tidal times	In West Loch Tarbert: The ingoing stream starts about 5 hrs and 40 mins after HW Ullapool. The outgoing stream starts about 30 mins before HW Ullapool.
Tidal rates	The tidal streams here are almost imperceptible.
Coastguard	Stornoway, tel:01851 702013, VHF Weather 0710 UT

Introduction

Taransay is another Hebridean gem of an island. The steep rugged hills made of Lewisian Gneiss look inhospitable, but this island used to have a population large enough for a school. The Vikings were here, leaving their mark in the way of hill names; Herraval and Bullaval on Aird Vanish, and before that prehistoric man was on Taransay. Caves, sandy beaches, views to Harris and a sense of peace and quiet make this trip a great day out.

Description

Loch Leosavay is a small quiet loch that will often mask the true state of the sea further out. Atlantic salmon enter this loch looking for the river that runs up to Lochan Beag; their journey up this steep river can be nothing but exhausting as it has a series of steps which they have to jump up on their way to the spawning beds further upstream. Taransay had successfully escaped the limelight until the year 2000, when the BBC decided to use the island for a social experiment. 36 people were selected to live together as a community on this island that last had residents in 1974. The ups and downs of living together were aired on the television for millions to view. They were housed in buildings especially made for the programme called 'pods'. 29 of the original 36 'Castaways' remained on Taransay for the full experiment, lasting one year. Due to the placing of Taransay on the map by this programme, people want to come and visit the island, so now you can more easily get a boat to take you over for a day trip and there are also 2 holiday lets available on Taransay.

The island is still a working farm, the farmer lives on Harris and comes across to Taransay to look after his sheep and cattle.

The island is named after Saint Taran and there is a chapel site called St Taran's where women were buried and not far away another chapel site known as St Keith's where only men were buried. These chapel sites are very close to Paibeil on the promontory of Rubha nan Sgarbh, named after the shags that perch on the rocks here. The isthmus at the head of Loch na h-Uidhe is a glorious stretch of the cleanest white sand. In the dunes where the wind and sea have eroded away some of the sand you can see shells that were cast up into the dunes by storms of times long gone by.

Going round Aird Mhanais you can explore caves and pass through an arch. Take another break to soak up the afternoon sun on Traigh a' Siar, as this will more than likely be your last stop before starting the journey home. Up on the hillside to the east of this fine beach you will see 'lazy beds', raised strips of ground with runnels between them where people used to grow their crops. The thin soil meant that to get enough depth you had to take the soil from one bit and place it on top of the adjacent ground; a by-product of this is that a good run-off channel is made for the excess rain to drain away, leaving the soil less waterlogged. To improve the fertility of the thin soil, seaweed would have been gathered and taken to the lazy beds; all in all making crops grow in this manner was not a job for the lazy.

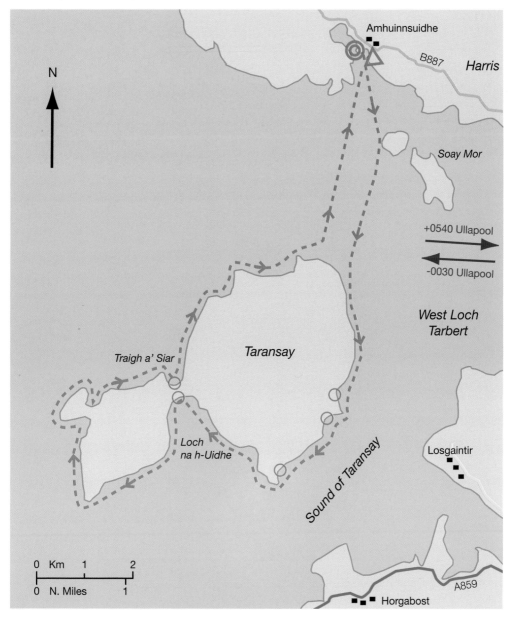

On the journey back over West Loch Tarbert toward the islands of Soay Beg and Soay Mor, the sheep islands, you will have the high peak of Cleiseval 511m as a back drop, and behind this the well-known cliff on Sron Ulladale looms. Here rock climbers pit their strength and technique against a climb known as 'The Scoop', a very difficult aid climb for most, but for those able to climb E6 there is a free climb described as "A serious and committing climb of awe-inspiring steepness".

Tide & Weather

With the tidal streams flowing gently in this area the weather might be the biggest hazard. The mountains of Harris to the north and east can produce significant down draughts when a wind comes from the N or NE.

Additional Information

It is a wee bit further to drive but if you haven't been here before it is well worth the extra time to see the view over to Scarp and to check out the sea state in Hushinish Bay.

Parking is limited at the little slipway beside the holiday cottage just above the water. If an alternative is needed, go along the road toward the post office in Amhuinnsuidhe.

Scarp

No. 32 | Grade B | 14km | 4 Hours | OS Sheet 13 | Tidal Port Ullapool

Start	△ Hushinish Pier (989124)
Finish	◎ Hushinish Pier (989124)
HW/LW	HW/LW in Braigh Mor (997167) is about 55 minutes before Ullapool.
Tidal times	Around Gasker, which is 8km to the SW of Scarp The N going stream starts about 4 hrs and 30 mins before HW Ullapool. The S going stream starts about 1 hr and 55 mins after HW Ullapool.
Tidal rates	The average spring rate off Gasker is around 2 knots.
Coastguard	Stornoway, tel:01851 702013, VHF Weather 0710 UT

Introduction

If you are lucky enough to arrive here when the machair is in full bloom and the gannets are diving into Caolas an Scarp with the beautiful clean sands to the north, you might be excused for just wanting to lie amongst the flowers in a sea of colour soaking up the sun.

Don't be tempted! This is a wonderful place to paddle. The air is nowhere cleaner, the sea nowhere clearer.

The beautiful machair of Hushinish

Description

Hushinish Bay has a magnificent sandy beach which can be used as an alternative start. Watch out though, this is another place where you might be seduced by its charm and never get started, choosing to sunbathe the hours away. Between Hushinish Bay and the pier, half a kilometre to the north is a beautiful machair, rich in colour when it is in full bloom.

Scarp at one time was the most westerly island in the UK that had a resident population. Numbers peaked on this island in 1881 with just over 200 people living on this rough westerly outpost. As with much of the surrounding land, Scarp is made of gneiss, a hard metamorphic rock that is only just covered by a thin smear of soil. There are easier places to live but that is what people did. Some of the people displaced by the clearances on North Harris settled on Scarp.

The south and west shore of Scarp is rough, being fully exposed to the relentless winter storms from the Atlantic. About a kilometre round the coast from Rubha na Creadha is Mol Mor; the stream that runs down into this bay from Loch Uidemul once powered the millstones that the islanders used to grind their grain. The site of the old mill is close to where the ageing millstones lie about 200m up from the shore. About halfway along the SW coast is a little promontory called Manish, inland from here there is an unusual rock, known as 'the asbestos rock'.

On the north coast there are two islands Ostem and Kearstay, Kearstay was used to keep some young sheep during the winter months. Opposite Kearstay is a small sandy beach where a break can be taken.

Off the east coast of Scarp is the small island of Fladday where peat used to be cut and rams grazed, thereby keeping them away from the ewes.

It was across the narrow channel of Caolas an Scarp that a German scientist chose to test his rocket that would conveniently take the post from Scarp to Harris when the sea was too rough for the mailboat to sail. His first attempt failed, resulting in all the mail being scattered over the foreshore of Scarp as the rocket exploded. At a second attempt he achieved success, but his idea never caught on.

The south-east corner of Scarp is where the deserted village stands, with its pier, burial ground and old school, which closed in 1967.

Unfortunately, Scarp has seen its fair share of land speculation over the years where companies or individuals buy parts of Scotland looking for a profit through doing nothing more than selling it on again at a higher price. A good example of this was when the island was sold one February for £50,000 and less than 2 months later was sold for £500,000. At one time there was talk of developing Scarp into a tourist resort; fortunately an old feudal burden prohibits the development of tourism on the island and therefore peace and quiet has been preserved.

Tide & Weather

There is not much precise tidal information available for the shores of Scarp, so it would be good to be open-minded about what will be happening. Choosing a calm sea without much swell, light winds and a period of neap tides will go a long way to minimising any hard work that is associated with paddling against a tidal stream.

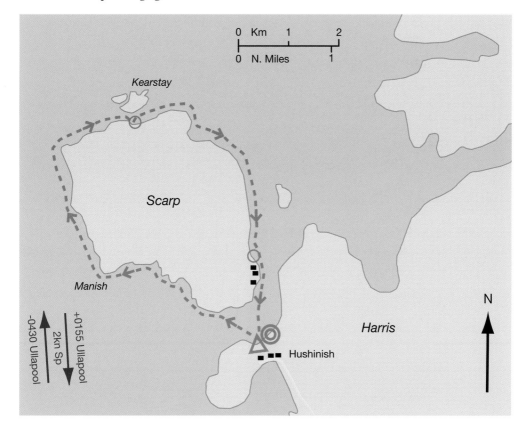

32

Scarp

Standing Stones

Along with brochs, standing stones are creations of a period some 3000 years ago. The standing stones pictured here at Callanish on the west coast of Lewis in the Outer Hebrides are one of the best examples in Scotland. The largest of the stones, approximately 5m high, stands in the middle of the other stones which are arranged in a cross shape. Why such large stones were used and for what purpose remains a topic of debate. The visitor centre beside the Stones of Callanish provides the most up-to-date information on such structures. The stones themselves are made of an ancient hard metamorphic rock known as Lewisian Gneiss, this rock has a distinctive appearance with alternating light and dark bands of minerals waving their way through the rock. If you take the west coast route up to the Butt of Lewis, Trip 33, you will pass this superb site and a further 10km north there is the impressive Dun Carloway broch.

Additional Information

The pier is still used by locals who fish in these waters and farm sheep on the island of Scarp, so please park your car sensitively.

If you can arrange the transport, a fantastic trip to do along one of the remotest sections of the Scottish coast is to go northwards from Hushinish Pier, passing Scarp, Mealasta Island and the superb cliffs at Ard More Mangersta, finishing at Uig Sands, in total a 26km trip from Hushinish.

Butt of Lewis

No. 33 | Grade B | 20km | 5 Hours | OS Sheet 8 | Tidal Port Ullapool

Start	△ Port of Ness (539637)
Finish	◎ Traigh Sands, Eoropie (512646)
HW/LW	HW/LW at Stornoway is about 10 minutes before Ullapool.
Tidal times	Round the Butt of Lewis: The stream that comes north up the west coast turns east round the Butt and then heads south-east down the east coast of Lewis, and starts about 4 hrs 45 mins before HW Ullapool. The stream that comes north up the east coast turns west round the Butt and then heads south-west down the west coast of Lewis, starting about 1 hr 40 mins after HW Ullapool. When the tidal stream runs SW down the west coast, an eddy runs back NE toward the Butt of Lewis.
Tidal rates	Off the Butt of Lewis the average spring rate is around 5 knots.
Coastguard	Stornoway, tel:01851 702013, VHF Weather 0710 UT

Introduction

This is it, 'The End', and it certainly feels close to the end when you are being tossed about in the froth below the lighthouse!

The Butt of Lewis is one of the windiest places in Great Britain and is also one of Scotland's major landmarks. For many it was not the end but the start of a new beginning. Thousands of Scots passed this way emigrating across the Atlantic; some would have been forced by the consequences of the 'Clearances' where landlords replaced people with sheep and then deer. Others would be emigrating through choice; either way sadness must have swept through the passengers as they lost sight of their homeland.

Description

A trip round the Butt from Port of Ness to Eoropie is relatively short, so it is worthwhile doing a little trip as a prelude down the east coast to Cladach Cuiashader, here there is a fine little beach to haul up on and sunbathe for a while. The trip down is a fine journey past natural arches, skerries and colourful cliffs.

Port of Ness is where the locals sail from on their annual journey in the autumn up to Sula Sgeir, a tiny island 70km to the NNE, where they harvest young gannets (guga), which are considered a delicacy in Lewis.

If you were to see dolphins here they might be Risso's dolphins, a largish grey coloured dolphin about 3.5m long with no beak and often seen with scars on its back.

The lighthouse designed by David Stevenson, who was the grandfather of Robert Louis Stevenson, stands at 37m in height. It is built of red bricks so looks a bit dull in comparison to many of the whitewashed lighthouses round our coast. Originally the light, first lit in 1862, was produced from fish oil, then paraffin and latterly electricity. In 1998 the lighthouse saw the departure of the last keeper when it became fully automated. Today it serves the dual purposes of warning mariners with its light, which can be seen from 40km away, and acting as a transmitting station for differential GPS. Due to the difficulty of transport to such a remote spot, the lighthouse was originally serviced by sea; boats used the small inlet at Port Stoth, which lies 0.5km SE of the lighthouse.

About a kilometre after the lighthouse there is a tiny island called Luchruban with a chambered building on its summit. It is known as the island of little people, and is said to be the last refuge

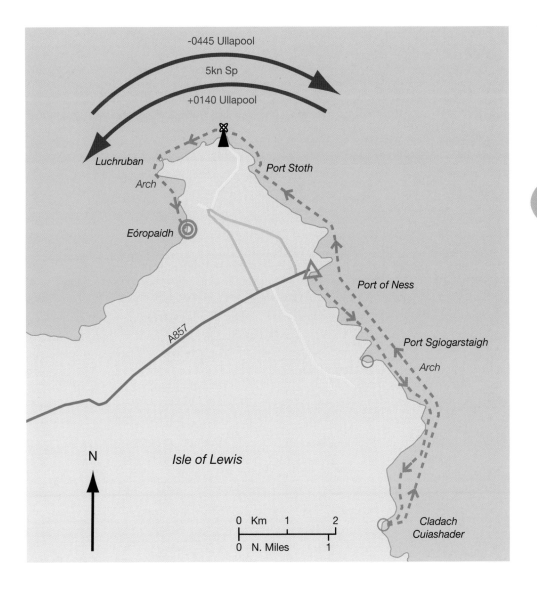

Close to Cladach Cuiashader

of a race of pygmies that lived on Lewis. Excavations on the island revealed bones of animals and birds but no human bones to support the legend that pygmies used to inhabit the area.

Tide & Weather

The tidal streams in this area are very strong. The skerries off the Butt ensure that the fast tidal streams are even further squeezed and contorted out of line, therefore the sea here rarely lies still. Landing at Traigh Sands could be exciting if there is a bit of a swell running, watch out for the rip at the north end of the beach.

Make every effort to be at the Butt of Lewis when the stream is due to run west at around 1 hour 40 minutes after HW Ullapool. Remember, it is not unusual for tidal streams to run earlier or indeed later than previously recorded times.

Leaving, or passing Port of Ness about 1 hour after HW Ullapool should mean that you arrive at the Butt as the tidal streams change direction.

Additional Information

It is worth going to Eoropie before setting out just to check the state of the sea on the west coast, especially the size of the surf, even to the extent of going down to the beach to check out the landing options close up.

Dun Carloway

Brochs

As you travel around the west coast, take the time to search out one of these magnificent structures. Brochs were probably built in the period 1000BC to 1000AD, as fortifications to retreat into when there was a danger of attack. They look like industrial cooling towers, but they are far more attractive and interesting. The entire structure is made of stone, not bonded with mortar, just dry stones expertly laid and capable of surviving centuries of storms. The ruinous state of many of the brochs is in part due to people having taken stones to build houses after the period when brochs were needed for protection. They were constructed without the need for scaffolding despite standing at 10m or more in height; this was made possible by the design of hollow walls, with a staircase between the inner and outer walls. There is only one entrance into a broch, and there are no windows, so in the days when these fantastic structures were built, the only way to overpower the occupants of a broch was to be patient and wait till the occupants ran out of food and water. This could be a long time as the broch would have been stocked with supplies prior to being attacked and there was room inside to hold animals as well as people. If you are travelling north to Lewis, having paddled any of the trips on Harris (Trips 30,31 & 32), make the effort to visit Dun Carloway which is over on the west coast of Lewis about 10km north of the standing stones at Callanish. Having visited these two historic sites the next trip north is Trip 33 - Butt of Lewis, about 40km to the NE from Dun Carloway.

Approaching the Butt of Lewis

Shiant Isles

No. 34 | **Grade C** | **Day 1 - 30km/7-8 hrs** | **Day 2 - 40 or 30km/10hrs + ferry or 7-8hrs to Tarbert** | **OS Sheet 14 & 23** | **Tidal Port Ullapool**

Start	△ Camas Mor (370706)
Finish	◎ Camas Mor (370706) or Tarbert (157998)
HW/LW	HW/LW the Shiants is around 20 minutes before Ullapool.
Tidal times	For Ru Bornesketaig off Camas Mor:

For Ru Bornesketaig off Camas Mor:
The NE going stream starts about 4 hrs 15 mins before HW Ullapool.
The SW going stream starts about 2 hrs 10 mins after HW Ullapool.

For the Shiant Isles off the S end:
The NE going stream starts about 3 hrs and 30 mins before HW Ullapool.
There is slack water at about 1 hr and 40 mins after HW Ullapool.
The SW going stream starts about 2 hrs 55 mins after HW Ullapool.

For the Shiant Sound:
The NE going stream starts about 3 hrs 15 mins before HW Ullapool.
The SW going stream starts about 3 hrs 10 mins after HW Ullapool.

For the Sound of Scalpay:
The E going stream starts about 5 hrs 30 mins before HW Ullapool.
The W going stream starts about 55 mins after HW Ullapool.

Natural arch, Eilean Garbh, Shiant Isles

Tidal rates	There are four areas on this trip where the tidal streams run at their fastest:
	Off the N and S ends of Fladda-chuain the average spring rate can reach 2.5 knots.
	Off the S end of the Shiants the average spring rate can reach 3 knots.
	In the Sound of Shiant the average spring rate can reach 2.5 knots.
	In the Sound of Scalpay the average spring rate can reach 2 knots.
Coastguard	Stornoway, tel: 01851 702013, VHF Weather 0710 UT

Introduction

To set off from Skye and cross the Minch to the Outer Hebrides has got to be one of the classic crossings. Add to this the islands off the North of Skye along with the unique Shiant Isles and this is without a doubt a remarkable paddle. With the option of continuing on from the Shiants to Tarbert and getting the ferry back, you have your perfect journey. For this trip to be successful it will take careful weather watching for the right conditions and good tidal planning to make it as easy as possible. The time spent on this will make the trip one to remember.

Description

When setting off from the small pier at Camas Mor there will always be a feeling of apprehension. "Will the weather hold, and have the tides been worked out correctly" will be part of it but "Will I need to go to the toilet on the 3 hour crossing to the Shiants" will be the main concern! Leave Camas Mor and head for the rocky island of An t-Iasgair where there is no landing, but good rock architecture and plenty of nesting kittiwakes, puffins, guillemots and razorbills. From here you will have the tide at your back and gain a gentle push for the 6km to Fladda-chuain; watch out for large boats and submarines as this channel is often used. Before heading to the only easy landing spot halfway up the west side of the islands where there is a small ruined house and stone cleared landing inlet, consider exploring the other islands. Lord Macdonald's Table is a must with a natural arch separating it from Gearran Island. Having rested and explored the wildlife of Fladda-chuain (look out for the big black rabbits), you'll be ready to head to the Shiant Isles you can hopefully see in the distance.

With some help from the tide and hopefully the weather, the crossing should take no more than three hours. With the expanse of the Western Isles arcing from back left to dead ahead and the disappearing Skye and mainland behind, the time will soon pass. As the grand sentinels of the Shiant Isles come into closer view, so will the number of puffins increase around you, and the calls of thousands of seabirds will soon be heard from the islands. As you reach the towering sides of

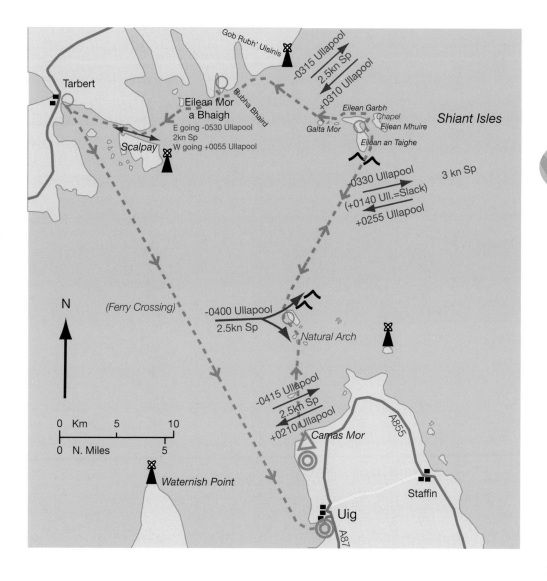

Eilean an Taighe, Shiant Isles

the southern island of the Shiants, Eilean an Taighe, head up to the isthmus where it joins Garbh Eilean to land. The eastern side gives the most shelter and from here there is good camping on the northern tip of Eilean an Taighe. The locked hut used by the sheep farmer when visiting the island is also found here. If spending the night camping there are rats on the island, so make sure nothing edible is left outside. To spend some time exploring the island on foot is well worth the effort, as you will be amazed by the amount of crofts scattering the hillside, which housed up to five families until 1901. Since then it has been uninhabited. Paddling around the other islands which make up the Shiants you will be rewarded with a wealth of bird life, seals, impressive basalt cliffs and arches. In itself it is a memorable paddle and if you can manage the rocky landing required, then landing on Eilean Mhuire will offer more of the history of the Shiants. This is the most fertile of the islands and again has many remnants of former habitation, of particular interest is the ruined chapel dedicated to the Virgin Mary.

Leaving the Shiants you may be heading back across the Minch to Skye, or a recommended option would be to continue to Tarbert. This route would take you past Galta Mor, the most westerly of the Shiants, and across the Sound of Shiant to Harris, which is the more mountainous southern half of the Isle of Lewis. Again planning to make the best use of the tide helps and the headland of Rubh a Bhaird is a good place to aim for. This then gives options for landing in the inlets to the west of the headland. From here paddling down the Harris coastline will give the sense of remoteness that the Western Isles have. Paddling past Eilean Mor a Bhaigh and on underneath the bridge in the Sound of Scalpay will take you into East Loch Tarbert. You may wish to pull into the naturally sheltered North Harbour of Scalpay for a rest, or if you are catching the ferry then the final paddle into Tarbert will be beckoning.

Bothy, Eilean an Taighe

You can carry your kayak aboard the ferry, usually paying the charge for a bicycle, and then it will be a relaxing journey back to Skye. En route you will be able to trace where you have paddled, with the Shiants looking distant to the north. On arriving in Uig, it is a short drive back to Camas Mor, or if time and fitness allow then two hours should see you comfortably back there by kayak.

Tide & Weather

To carry out this trip some detailed tidal planning will be required. It is best to leave Camas Mor at the start of the NE stream, 4 hours 15 minutes before HW Ullapool. From Ru Bornesketaig to An t- Iasgair a slight ferry glide will be required, then use the tide to take you up to Fladda-chuain. For the crossing to the Shiants it is best to time it so as to arrive at the Shiants at slack water, 1 hour 40 minutes after HW Ullapool, so that the sea state will be easy for a tired paddler at the end of a three hour crossing. Timing it like this means that you will have to paddle through the tidal race which forms off the north end of Fladda-chuain and will push you in a NE direction if you are not careful. On neap tides however it is certainly not a violent race and is no more than a few hundred metres wide. It is worth considering using tidal vectors for the crossing to get most effect from the tide, and paddle no further than required. There is a useful tidal diamond on the chart to help with this, however on neap tides the drift is not too great if vectors were not used, but I would still recommend it.

If returning to Skye from the Shiants it would be worth leaving at about slack and then using the first 3 hours of the SW stream, which starts 2 hours 55 minutes after HW Ullapool, to return to Fladda-chuain. This will then give you the tide to continue down to Camas Mor, but again being aware of the tidal race at the north end of Fladda-chuain, this time setting off in a more NW direction.

Shiant Isles, Harris in the backgound

If continuing on to Tarbert you will want to leave the Shiants towards the start of the SW stream which starts at about 3 hours 10 minutes after HW Ullapool. Crossing Shiant Sound to reach Harris will again be best done considering the use of vectors to make the most efficient crossing with the tide. On the chart there is another useful tidal diamond to help with this. Once across the sound there is negligible tidal movement until the Sound of Scalpay is reached. The tidal stream in this sound can run up to 2 knots on an average spring tide and starts to run E at about 5 hours and 30 minutes before HW Ullapool. This is only in the narrows however, and as it may be hard to plan the trip to arrive before it starts running east, then it is relatively easy to eddy hop up the narrows even on a spring tide.

Due to the nature of the trip and the crossings generally going slightly across the tidal streams, it is worth considering this trip on neap tides for best results. It is also clear that this trip takes in some very exposed water, so a settled spell of weather with minimal winds is also required.

Additional Information

To get information and timetables for the Tarbert-Uig Ferry contact Caledonian MacBrayne Ferries on www.calmac.co.uk.

The Shiant Isles are owned by the Nicolson family and there is a good book called 'Sea Room an Island Life' by Adam Nicolson, about their history. In planning this trip, using the Admiralty Chart 1794, North Minch – Southern Part is worthwhile.

Cape Wrath

No. 35 | Grade C | Day 1 - 25km/6 hrs | Day 2 - 16km/4 hrs | OS Sheet 9 | Tidal Port Ullapool

Start	△ Balnakeil (391687)
Finish	◎ Kinlochbervie (217564)
HW/LW	HW/LW at Kinlochbervie is about 15 minutes after Ullapool.
Tidal times	From Stac Clo Kearvaig (294736) eastwards: The E going stream starts about 2 hrs and 20 mins before HW Ullapool. The W going stream starts about 3 hrs and 50 mins after HW Ullapool.
	From Cape Wrath to Stac Clo Kearvaig: The E going stream starts about 3 hrs and 50 mins before HW Ullapool. The W going stream starts about 2 hrs and 35 mins after HW Ullapool.
	From Cape Wrath down to Eilean an Roin Beag (172583): The NE going stream starts about 1 hr and 20 mins before HW Ullapool. The SW going stream starts about 4 hrs and 55 mins after HW Ullapool.
Tidal rates	At Cape Wrath itself, expect rates of up to 5kns. To the east of Cape Wrath, close in to the coast along to Stack Clo Kearvaig the rate is about 3kns. Further east at An Garbh-eilean the rate is also 3kns. To the south of Cape Wrath the rate of the tidal streams are less noticeable.

Kearvaig Bay

Very close in to the cliffs on either side of Cape Wrath there might be noticeable eddies. On the outside of Eilean an Roin Beag and between it and the mainland there is a noticeable tidal stream, the rate of which is not known.

Coastguard   Aberdeen (for the area E of Cape Wrath), tel:01224 592334, VHF Weather 0730 UT
Stornoway (for the area S of Cape Wrath), tel:01851 702013, VHF Weather 0710 UT

Introduction

Cape Wrath, the furthest NW point on the Scottish mainland is a wild place. A lighthouse stands on the headland above the caves and arches where the sea swirls and boils as it forces its way around the headland on its journey from the west coast of Scotland to the north coast and back again. The highest sea cliffs on the mainland are here at Clo Mor, 600 vertical feet of unclimbed rock. In amongst this rugged coastline are two beautiful sandy beaches, Kearvaig on the north coast and the very well known, much photographed, Sandwood Bay on the west coast.

Description

Balnakeil Bay is a superb place to start, the wonderfully clean, sandy beach stretches for 2km to the north and the water is crystal clear.

Once on the other side of the bay, the cliff scenery that will dominate this trip begins. When you pass through the gap between An Garbh-eilean and Cleit Dhubh the view to Clo Mor opens up, 3km of sea cliff stretching up to almost 200m in height. At the western end of Clo Mor stands Stac Clo Kearvaig, a popular place for breeding birds such as guillemots and razorbills. The stack is 40m high and was first climbed in 1989; if you look to the top of the stack you might see some old rope left wrapped around the summit spikes by climbers who descended by abseil.

The sandy beach of Kearvaig is just around the corner and a stop here would be advisable as the next opportunity to land more than likely will be Sandwood Bay. There is an open bothy up behind the beach where, if you so wished, you could spend the night. As well as resting and refuelling here, it provides a good opportunity to time your arrival at Cape Wrath to suit the tidal streams.

About halfway along to Cape Wrath from Kearvaig Bay is the jetty that was used by the Lighthouse Tender MV Pharos. This brought supplies on an annual basis for the lighthouse keepers before it was fully converted to an automatic lighthouse in 1998. This lighthouse, as with many others, is now remotely monitored from the offices of the Northern Lighthouse Board in Edinburgh.

Underneath the headland there is a large arch which, if the sea is not too rough, you will be able to pass through, the roughness in part comes from the fact that there is a tidal stream running through this arch.

A' Chailleach and Am Bodach are sea stacks situated just less than 2km south of Cape Wrath, and both have been ascended by rock climbers. A' Chailleach, 'the old woman', is the impressive slender stack which can only be gained by swimming out to, whereas Am Bodach, 'the old man', can be reached on foot at low water.

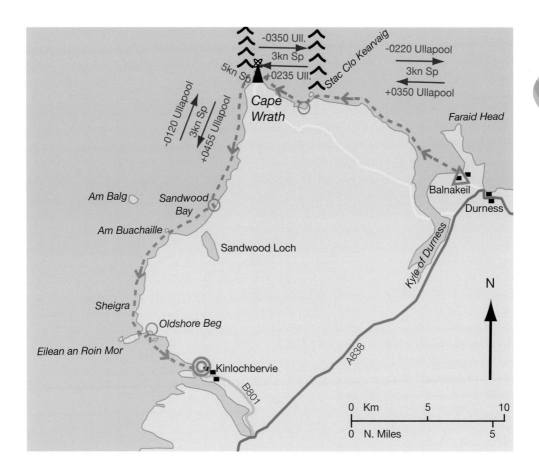

The first of the Kervaig stacks

The coastline continues southward with cliffs less spectacular than those on the north coast, but nonetheless a fine bit of coast. Am Buachaille, the most impressive sea stack on the trip will be seen to the south at the far end of Sandwood Bay.

Getting ashore at Sandwood Bay has got the potential to be exciting if there is a bit of swell running. It might be possible to land in smaller surf toward the top end of the bay close to where the river coming down Strath Chailleach flows into the sea. There is a small flat area at the top of a grassy slope rising above this beach where a tent can be pitched. Water can be taken from a small stream just metres away to the south. If you do land and camp at Sandwood Bay, watch out for the quicksand which is to be found between Sandwood Loch and the sea.

Am Buachaille is accessed by crossing an 8m stretch of water at low tide; once across the climbers have a window of 4 hours in which to climb the 50m stack before it becomes isolated by a large section of water. The coast continues with interest south to Eilean an Roin Mor where, passing through the narrow channel, you might experience the last of the moving water on this trip between it and the mainland. Turning to the north-east once through the channel brings you to a fine sandy beach below the village of Oldshore Beg.

Kinlochbervie is one of the most important white fish ports in Scotland. Rather than going into Loch Bervie with the large pier, land at the head of Loch Clash to the west of the town.

Tide & Weather

This is not a section of coastline to get caught out on. There are few landing spots on this rocky, remote bit of coast. If you do land to escape the sea then it probably will be a fair old hike to reach a road. The headland of Cape Wrath is fully exposed to the Atlantic and rarely will there be a day

Lazy Beds

Quite often when you are travelling along the remoter parts of the west and north of Scotland you will see these parallel ridges and ditches on the hillsides. They are evidence that the thin, wet soils of our rugged coast used to provide people with food. Potatoes, oats or corn would have been cultivated on these ridges. The soil was more often than not very poor in nutrients as well as being shallow. To make a decent bed for the plants to grow, seaweed (as a fertilizer) was laid in strips and then the adjacent turf was laid on top, thereby creating alternating ditches and ridges. The ditches served to allow the excessive rain to drain away, leaving the ridges and the plants less waterlogged than they might otherwise be.

without much swell; which ever direction it comes from it will have an effect on how this trip goes. The ideal conditions would be a very light easterly or north-easterly wind, with no swell running on either coast.

Leaving very early in the morning, if the tides allow, from Balnakeil would provide you with sunlight shining on the cliffs on the way out to Cape Wrath, great for photographs.

Due to the nature of the complicated tidal streams, eddies and the exposure, plan to do this trip during neaps so that, if you end up going against a stream, it should never be that strong.

As a rough guide, if you leave Balnakeil about 1 hour after HW Ullapool, you should reach Cape Wrath as the SW going stream starts at 4 hours and 55 minutes after HW Ullapool.

Cape Wrath

Additional Information

Cape Wrath is a Live Firing Exercise Area for the military. Check with the coastguard, look in local papers, check at the shop in Durness and look to see if any red flags are flying before you set off.

Caves on the west side of Whiten Head

Whiten Head

No 36 | **Grade C** | **27km** | **7 Hours** | **OS Sheet 9 & 10** | **Tidal Port Ullapool**

Start	△ Talmine (586627)
Finish	◎ Ard Neackie (448597)
HW/LW	HW/LW at Loch Eriboll is around 3 hours and 7 minutes before Wick.
Tidal times	Off Whiten Head: The W going stream starts about 3 hrs and 50 mins after HW Ullapool. The E going stream starts about 2 hrs and 20 mins before HW Ullapool.
Tidal rates	The tidal stream is at its fastest off Whiten Head. Here the average spring rate can reach 3 knots.
Coastguard	Aberdeen, tel:01224 592334, VHF Weather 0730 UT

Introduction

There can be few places in Britain that offer as remote and committing a day's paddle as Whiten Head. With next to no landings, the expanse of the Atlantic Ocean on one side and 250m cliffs on the other, it really is an incredible environment. There is little room for error on this trip, but that in itself makes it a paddle that has to be done.

Description

The sandy beach and harbour starting point at Talmine is as picturesque a put-in as you could ask for. It is nicely sheltered and is of total contrast to the environment not far around the corner. As you head off along the first few kilometres to the beach at Strathan, you may start feeling the ocean come alive underneath your boat. It is then that any swell and tide will start to be experienced. The beautiful sandy beach at Strathan is too early for lunch, but if any last minute adjustments are needed, be sure to stop as it might be up to 15km before another stop is possible. On leaving this beach the imposing cliffs leading to Whiten Head start to grow in magnitude. As you pass the rocky bay of Geodha Brat and paddle on to Rubha Thormaid, the rock and grass cliff sides rise up to 250m above. The rock walls are made up of metamorphic gneiss, and provide fantastic shapes and contortions amongst the rock features. Soon you will see the steeply shelving pebble beach of Geodha nan Aigheann; in calm seas this gives the only possible landing place on this headland. Once ashore, the inaccessible beach is surrounded by imposing steep sides of rock and grass. The only things escaping from this area are the seabirds that circle above.

Continuing on there are sea stacks and tempting arches, but rarely is the sea calm enough to explore them. The mountain-like Cleit an t-Seabhaig dominates the view as you pass it on the way to the head. As you round Whiten Head the views are fantastic, in front are ornate sea stacks climbing out of the sea, and in the background is Cape Wrath standing proud out into the Atlantic Ocean. Having enjoyed the sea stacks you round the corner to find a cathedral of a cave. If lucky enough to have the conditions to enter there are a choice of ways in and out, with the ceiling high above your head and the sea echoing around you . The rock changes in this area as well and with the afternoon sun it will glow yellow in colour. Entering the mouth of Loch Eriboll the cliffs lose their grandeur and landing places become available on the rocky shoreline. Although not as grand, the cliffs still have plenty of hidden surprises, with further caves and arches all the way down to the navigation light. If you have time to stretch your legs, the bothy at Freisgill is a unique resting spot. Passing under the light at low spring tides might allow you to see 'dead man's fingers', an orange coloured soft coral that lives on the rock walls. From here you can see the final few kilometres to the sheltered landing at the Lime Kilns of Ard Neackie. This provides an easy landing to reflect on a big day of paddling some of Scotland's remotest coastline.

Tide & Weather

Whiten Head is very exposed to swell from the west, north and east, as well as the wind. There are no easy landings and certainly no escape routes. With this in mind good weather conditions are best, from a safety and enjoyment point of view.

To make good use of the tidal stream on this journey it is best to paddle it with the west-going stream, which starts about 3 hours and 50 minutes after HW Ullapool. Once around Whiten Head the tidal streams are negligible so allowing 4 hours of west-going stream will be plenty to reach the head from Talmine. This would mean leaving Talmine at no later than 5 hours and 50 minutes after HW Ullapool. Leaving anything up to 2 hours earlier than this would just give more time to play with.

If the tidal times do not work, then beginning at Ard Neackie at the start of the east-going stream, 2 hours and 20 minutes before HW Ullapool, also works well.

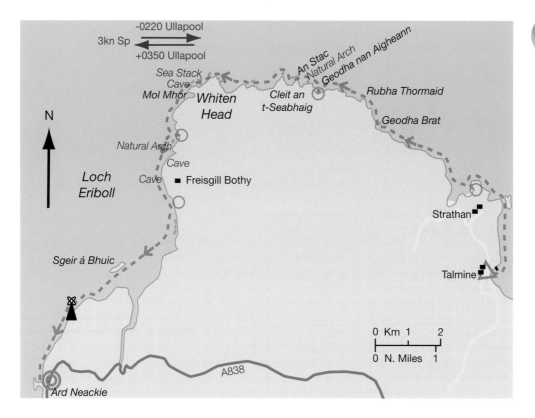

The impressive stacks of Whiten Head

Additional Information

Talmine has a full range of local amenities to enjoy at the start or finish of the day.

In this area under the cliffs VHF communications with Aberdeen can be difficult.

Eilean Nan Ron

No. 37 | Grade B | 20km | 6 Hours | OS Sheet 10 | Tidal Port Ullapool

Start	△ Skerray Pier (660637)
Finish	◎ Skerray Pier (660637)
HW/LW	HW/LW at Loch Eriboll is around 3 hours and 7 minutes before Wick.
Tidal times	For the main stream on the outside of the islands and in Caol Raineach: The W going stream starts about 3 hrs and 50 mins after HW Ullapool. The E going stream starts about 2 hrs and 20 mins before HW Ullapool. Between the Rabbit Islands and Eilean nan Ron: The S going stream starts about 2 hrs and 20 mins before HW Ullapool and only runs for 3.5 hours. The N going stream starts about 1 hr and 10 mins after HW Ullapool. In Kyle of Tongue and around Rabbit Isles: The outgoing stream starts about 1 hr and 10 mins after HW Ullapool. The ingoing stream starts about 5 hrs and 5 mins before HW Ullapool.
Tidal rates	The tidal stream is at its fastest between Eilean nan Ron and the mainland. Here the average spring rate can reach 2 knots.
Coastguard	Aberdeen, tel:01224 592334, VHF Weather 0730 UT

Introduction

This is a journey of contrasts in more ways than one. It offers committing exposed coastline with impressive cliffs and no landing, along with sheltered waters and sandy beaches. It has changing rock architecture and rock type at every corner. It has areas devoid of habitation, areas that used to be heavily populated now lying empty as a ghost town, and busy local fishing hamlets. This is a fantastic journey in which you can choose how much and where you want to paddle.

Description

Leaving the sheltered stony beach by Skerray harbour it is worth heading through Caol Beag around Neave Island. You will soon pass on the SE corner a stunning sandy beach, with maybe a lone seal sunbathing on it. This is the kind of beach you will just want to spend the day on, maybe another day, as the journey is well worth continuing. The intricate cliffs lead you round to an ornate arch on the northern tip of the island. Don't be tempted to cut across to Eilean nan Ron until you have discovered the large cave followed by a hidden arch inlet, around the next couple of corners.

Mol na Coinnle is the main landing spot to head for on Eilean nan Ron, and well worth the time for lunch. There is a unique, tiny natural harbour on the right as you enter the bay. At low water this has to be entered through a small natural arch, it then has steps leading up to the route to the settlement. In 1881 this settlement was at its largest with 8 houses and 73 habitants. There is no one living on the island these days and it is a National Nature Reserve with many grey seals using it to breed in the autumn. Moving on north from the harbour, a large natural arch leading into an open top cave will soon be passed. On the outside of the island a sense of the exposure of the north coast will be felt as you pass an arch over a rock slab where the islanders used to dry their fish. It is worth continuing on around Meall Thailm for the rock architecture and bird life, however a short cut to a landing spot is available between Mol Mor and Eilean Iosal up to about mid-tide when it dries.

For a shorter journey it is easy to head back from here, however if time and energy allow, the Rabbit Islands are worth the visit. Head to Sgeir an Oir and see if you can find the narrow natural arch which splits the island in two. On the calmest of days it is possible to paddle through this unique arch. If circumnavigating the islands take care on the shallow sandbars off the SW corner, but a landing on the immaculate sheltered beach on the south side is a must. From here there is the opportunity to explore the mainland coastline on the way back to Skerray, with yet more cliffs and inlets.

Tide & Weather

A good day's paddling will be possible in any reasonable weather conditions in this area. The outside of the islands is very exposed to the swell and the weather however, so only commit to these areas where there are no landings in fine conditions.

The tidal streams in this area are fairly complex, however even on spring tides they are never too fast. With this in mind it is possible to paddle this journey at any state of the tide, being aware that using the natural eddies of the islands en route could ease passage. It is quite easy to have the tide with you all the way, and if this is possible with the times of high water then it is recommended.

Leaving Skerray pier in the last 2-3 hours of the west-going stream (5 hours before HW Ullapool) you will enjoy the push of the tide all the way to Meall Thailm, including time for a stop

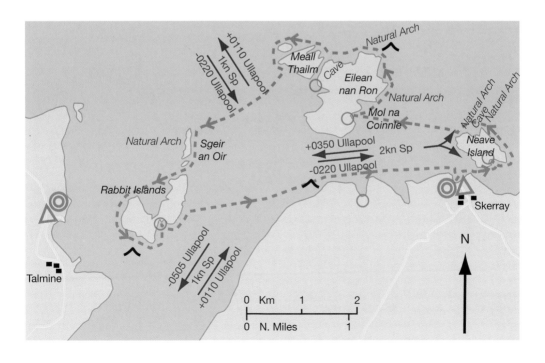

on Eilean nan Ron. Here you should pick up the start of the S going stream (2 hours 20 minutes before HW Ullapool) to take you down the Rabbit Islands. Leaving these islands, the crossing into Caol Raineach will be at the end of the Kyle of Tongue ingoing stream and you will pick up the E going stream through Caol Raineach to take you back to Skerray. So for the trip to work this way you will be looking for HW Ullapool to be around 15.00 hours. As already stated however, if this does not fit then it is possible to paddle without using the tidal streams to assist at any time.

It is worth noting that off the easternmost point of Eilean nan Ron the W going stream splits north and south around the island. This causes slightly faster and rougher water off the NE tip of the island in the W going tidal stream. Also within Caol Raineach, when the W going stream starts, rough water can occur on the south side of the channel as it meets the outgoing stream from the Kyle of Tongue.

Additional Information

The fishing village of Talmine opposite the Rabbit Islands makes a good alternative start and finish point. It has a shop, toilets and nice pub, along with easy landing, launching and car parking.

Strathy Point

No. 38 | Grade B | 15km | 4 Hours | OS Sheet 10 | Tidal Port Ullapool

Start	△ Armadale, Port a' Chinn (782651)
Finish	◎ Portskerra (878663)
HW/LW	HW/LW at Scrabster is about 2 hours and 40 minutes before Wick.
Tidal times	At Strathy Point:
	The E going stream starts about 2 hrs and 20 mins before HW Ullapool.
	The W going stream starts about 3 hrs and 50 mins after HW Ullapool.
Tidal rates	The average spring rate past Strathy Point is about 3 knots.
Coastguard	Aberdeen, tel:01224 592334, VHF Weather 0730 UT

Introduction

A fine quiet section of the Scottish coast, where the chances of meeting another kayaker on the water is very slim. The rocky coast has caves, arches, sandy bays and skerries to entertain the kayaker who has built in time to explore the coast between the start and the finish.

195

Description

Starting at Port a' Chinn is preferable as it is a bit of a walk down to the shore. It is not far in terms of horizontal distance but carrying your kayaks down the steep path is better than taking them up at the end of the day.

Where you park at the top of the cliff there is a fishing station, where nets are dried and cleaned. The fishermen have constructed a fantastic aerial cableway to get everything up and down between the shore and the top of the cliff. The bottom end of the cable is attached to a natural thread in the rock above the sea. This bay seems to be particularly well sheltered, the majority of any activity being quelled by the shape of the entrance and a few skerries.

The first bay round to the east is Armadale Bay, a bay of beautiful clean sand, which has no obvious footpath to it. Above the shore in amongst the close cropped grass, a flower unique to Scotland can be found, it is the Scottish Primrose, which has a small purple flower. The north coast is one of the few places where you will find this flower, which can bloom twice a year.

Geodh' Rubha below the unusually named group of houses called Brawl might give you a chance to land depending on the day. Port Allt a'Mhuilinn is the port below the stream that was used for a mill. If you go to explore up such streams it might be possible to find the remnants of old millstones.

If you are arriving early and want to kill some time before rounding Strathy Point, have a look into the small bay which is used by fishermen (823687), here a landing can be made depending on the height of the tide. The natural arch 500m before the lighthouse can be paddled under, but at most states of the tide it is not possible to do a round trip, you have to exit out the same way.

Strathy Point lighthouse was first lit in 1958 and is therefore a relative newcomer in comparison to the many lights that were made in the 1800's. It was the first all-electric station. As far back as 1900 requests were made for a lighthouse to be constructed here, and during the Second World War a temporary light was shown on this promontory. Prior to kayaking around this headland, it is well worthwhile coming to the lighthouse to get a feel for the place. It is possible to scramble about on the rocks right on the very tip of the point. Indeed, if you were here the day before a trip you could check the time and accuracy of the change in tidal stream direction.

Going south from the point toward Strathy Bay could be a bit slow going, as according to the pilot there is an almost continuous stream of water flowing northward along this coast.

From the 80m high cliffs just east of Strathy Bay to Portskerra the cliff scenery is interesting and colourful, with caves to explore. Climbers have established a few routes on the cliffs where the rock is sounder, close to Portskerra.

Portskerra used to be a busy harbour, used by many during the herring-fishing boom. It is a fantastic natural harbour with a concrete slipway to land beside. Here, at the end of August in

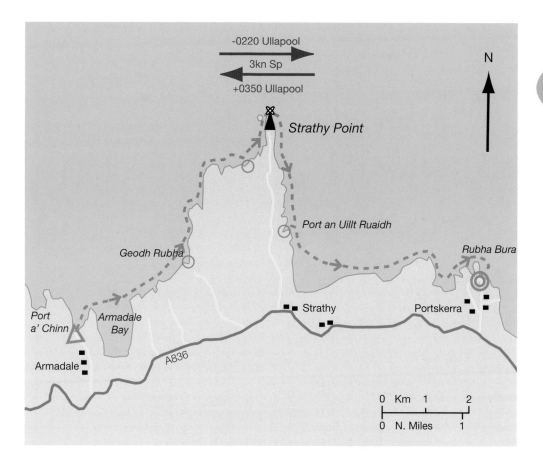

38

Surf Landing

The rhythmic gentle roll of an ocean swell played with my kayak as I paddled along the impressive cliffs alone. With only the ocean and wildlife for company I was at one with my surroundings and enjoying the solo experience. Strathy beach was around the corner and my lift would be waiting for me. As I rounded that corner there was an unmistakeable roar, which was confirmed by the huge plumes of spray making rainbows as they blew off the crests. The surf was massive and I stayed offshore to decide what to do. I could see my friend, waiting to pick me up, waving to me high on the cliffs, so at least there was someone to keep an eye on me. With heart pounding and palms sweating I paddled towards the surf zone. Timing frantic back-paddling to avoid huge waves as they started to pick up with equally frantic forward paddling in the lulls, I inched forward. Then out of nowhere I was picked up and thrown forward at a speed rarely experienced in a sea kayak. Spray was in my eyes as I fought for control, and then I was capsized and fighting to roll. Back upright I could make the final dash for the beach. As I walked up the shore looking back at the giant surf, two surf kayakers came to chat. They were friends from the Scottish Surf Team calling it a day because it was too big!

1918 a severe gale from the north-west appeared without warning, many men were out in their boats. It was a calm evening and they had cast their nets to catch the many herring when the storm took them by surprise. Seven of the Portskerra fishermen lost their lives that night, and by the time morning came the sea was calm once more.

Tide & Weather

When the tidal stream is running eastward past Strathy Point, it creates an eddy that runs northward on the east side of the headland. During spring tides this eddy and the natural flow of water northward during the period of the west going stream might be noticeable. Try to be at Strathy Point with an hour of the east-going stream left to run, this will be around 2 hours and 50 minutes after HW Ullapool.

As the tale of the Portskerra fishermen tells, watch out, the weather can change along this coast with little warning.

Duncansby Head and Stroma

No. 39 | Grade C | 24km | 6 Hours | OS Sheet 12 | Tidal Port Aberdeen

Start	△ Skirza Pier (386680)
Finish	◎ John o' Groats (379735)
HW/LW	HW/LW at Duncansby Head is about 1 hour and 10 minutes before Wick.
Tidal times	For Duncansby Head: The W going stream starts about 1 hr and 5 mins before HW Aberdeen. The E going stream starts about 5 hrs and 5 mins after HW Aberdeen. For Swilkie Point, Stroma: The E going stream starts about 5 hrs and 5 mins after HW Aberdeen. The W going stream starts about 1 hr and 20 mins before HW Aberdeen. In the Inner Sound: The E going stream starts about 4 hrs and 35 mins after HW Aberdeen. The W going stream starts about 1 hr and 50 mins before HW Aberdeen.
Tidal rates	There are three areas on this trip where the tides run fastest: Off Duncansby Head the average spring rate can reach 8 knots, between 'The Knee' and mainland it can reach speeds in excess of this. Off Swilkie Point the average spring rate can reach 9 knots. In the Inner Sound the average spring rate can reach 5 knots.
Coastguard	Aberdeen, tel:01224 592334, VHF Weather 0730 UT

Introduction

This is a journey never to be underestimated as it takes you into the notorious Pentland Firth. This trip passes through some of Britain's fastest tidal water in a part of the country that regularly attracts wild weather. Along with this it passes under huge cliffs, sea stacks and arches while being a haven for seabirds and mammals alike. On the right day with the right planning, this has got to be one of Scotland's most dramatic paddling venues.

Description

The tiny sheltered pier of Skirza where the trip starts is in total contrast to where the journey leads. As soon as Skirza Head is reached the sea will feel alive with tidal movement and this sets the tone for the day ahead. This initial small tidal flow subsides to give calm seas leading on to the Stacks of Duncansby. There are fantastic sandstone cliffs along this coastline with a mass of caves of all sizes lining the route. "Wife Geo" is soon passed, offering a huge, steep-sided inlet with caves around it. Continuing, the Stacks of Duncansby draw closer and their grandeur becomes ever more apparent. This grandeur has attracted climbers over the years, who have scaled their steep, and in places very loose, flanks. Having explored the stacks, continuing a short distance further brings you to a stony beach at Thirle Door. This is the last convenient place to land before the island of Stroma, so it is well worth stopping. Just around the corner from here is where the tide is squeezed into the Pentland Firth, originally named Pictland Firth from when the Picts were thought to have first settled on Orkney. To avoid the worst of the tidal races a wide route can be paddled out from the shore. If feeling brave it is well worth enjoying the races and possibly heading for the breakout behind 'The Knee'. This is a sea stack lying just 20m away from the vertical sandstone walls of Duncansby Head. The tide is squeezed between this gap at a fantastic speed, it is a great place to watch in awe or even play! As the speedy conveyer belt takes you on along these cliffs, be sure to break out into the Geo of Sclaites which is an awesome place to explore. Leaving here you round the headland and then, making careful use of the tidal streams, cross to the Nethertown pier on Stroma. This pier is guarded by a large community of grey seals, so be prepared to enjoy their company.

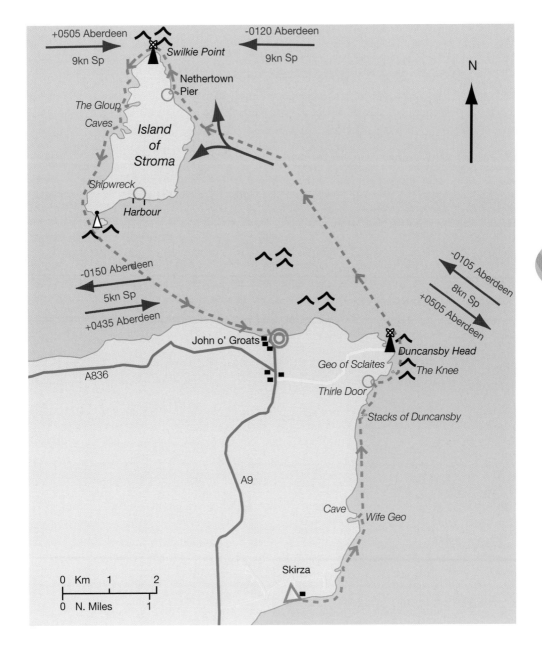

The Island of Stroma aptly translates from the Gaelic meaning 'island in the tidal stream'. Whilst enjoying a rest on the island you are clearly reminded of the harsh environment of this north coast. The island used to house 377 people and now lies deserted, only the shells of countless houses remain of this ghost town community today. Leaving the pier your timing should take you underneath the lighthouse at the northern end of the island marking the infamous Swilkie tidal race in relatively calm conditions. The west coast of Stroma is lined with further sandstone cliffs on which even more guillemots, razorbills, kittiwakes, fulmars and shags are nesting. Soon you will reach the incredible subterranean passage of 'The Gloup'. This is an amazing place to look at, but take a lot of care if venturing in as the narrow passage funnels and enlarges the slightest swell quite violently. There are further large caves as you continue on to Mell Head. Just before the head you will pass a shipwreck below Castle Mestag; look out for the iron bridge over the geo used by locals to access the wreck and retrieve things. From Mell Head it is time to jump back on the tidal conveyer belt, negotiate some rough water sometimes found around the old beacon, and paddle the last section to John o' Groats. If careful use of the tide has been made you will arrive in the tourist packed, yet sheltered harbour, in time to enjoy an ice cream.

Tide & Weather

Due to the exposed nature of this part of the world, the tidal streams and the committing nature of the route, this trip is not recommended in any other than perfect weather conditions.

The main tidal planning for this journey lies in using the west-going stream to reach Stroma, which starts at about 1 hour and 5 minutes before HW Aberdeen. To then get around Stroma it is essential to time it so as Swilkie Point is paddled around when the water is at its slackest, which in this case is just before the east-going stream starts at about 5 hours and 5 minutes after HW Aberdeen. The tidal streams in this area pick up speed very quickly, so do not leave it long after this otherwise it will not be possible to get around. Having paddled down the west coast of Stroma the east-going stream in the Inner Sound, which starts about 4 hours and 35 minutes after HW Aberdeen, will take you back to John o' Groats.

The tidal streams in this area are very strong so it is recommended to undertake this journey on neap tides initially. When crossing from Duncansby Head to Stroma the west-going stream splits around the island about halfway up the east coast. Make careful use of transits to ensure that you are not swept either south around the island or off to the north. Similarly when crossing back to John o' Groats it is best to head west of the pier so as to ensure it is not missed, again making careful use of transits.

Additional Information

There is limited parking at Skirza near a resident's house, so park courteously with as few vehicles as possible. There are regular ferries as well as larger ships using the Inner Sound so be aware of this and take care. In planning this trip, using the 1:50,000 Admiralty Chart 2162 Pentland Firth is worthwhile.

Noss Head

No. 40 | Grade A | 6km | 2 Hours | OS Sheet 12 | Tidal Port Aberdeen

Start	△ Ackergillshore (358545)
Finish	◎ Ackergillshore (358545)
HW/LW	HW/LW at Ackergillshore is about 2 hours and 20 minutes before Aberdeen.
Tidal times	Off Noss Head: The N going stream starts about 40 mins before HW Aberdeen. The S going stream starts about 5 hrs and 30 mins after HW Aberdeen.
Tidal rates	The average spring rate off Noss Head is about 1.75 knots.
Coastguard	Aberdeen, tel:01224 592334, VHF Weather 0730 UT

Introduction

This is a short trip, which is ideal for an evening paddle. The sun will be shining on the cliffs and the castles if you travel along this coast after 6pm during the summer. There are lots of caves to explore and a walk around the ruins of the two castles is very interesting.

Description

There is a fine wee harbour with a sandy bay from which to start. Parking close to the water is possible to reduce the distance you have to carry the kayak, but the end of the road is a turning spot and it might be better to park back up the road a bit.

At the start the land is quite low-lying and there are skerries, which keep you out from the shore a bit. If the wind is strong from the south there will be little shelter at this point; it is not until you travel a bit further along that you can come under the cliffs and have some protection from the wind.

The remains of our defences during the Second World War can be seen above the shore; a pillbox and a gun platform remain as evidence of uncertain times.

As soon as the cliffs start there are arches, stacks and caves to explore before you reach the castles. Castle Sinclair and Castle Girnigoe share the same small spit of land, which was obviously chosen for its ease of defence. If you go east of the castles you will find a hidden inlet, at the back of which you can land. As with all old buildings care must be taken if you choose to explore around the ruins. The way the first stones of the castle walls are laid and join onto the bedrock is very impressive; the joins are so good that they have withstood the battering of centuries better than the upper parts, which have succumbed to the elements. There is not much left of the older Castle Sinclair, but Castle Girnigoe still has high walls, windows and doorways through which you can explore.

Travelling further along the coast there are more caves, one with lime flows on the wall but no visible stalactites, and a stack which kittiwakes use to nest on.

There is a beach to land on just before you paddle under the cliff with the white wall of the lighthouse grounds. The lighthouse was first lit in June of 1849 and the original lamp is now kept in the Wick museum. The long road from Wick that provides access to the lighthouse was constructed by locals, who were otherwise unemployed, at the rate of 17 and a half pence a day.

In the light room hangs the following poem:

To Noss Head Light

As sweet to me as light of moon or star,
Is thy bright gleam, old trusty friend Noss Head
And doubly sweet, when o'er wide ocean far
The ray benignant on my course is shed
Blest be the hand that raised your steadfast tower
And he who trims you never-falling light
For oft when round me midnight tempests lower
Hope's pulse had failed, but for thy flash so bright
My gallant boat, though scare inch-thick her planks
Flies livelier on the track that heads her home
And dips her prow, as if in grateful thanks
When first your welcome ray reveals the billows foam
Long were the nights and weary were my watch
If from the lively deck thy flame I did not catch.

Travelling back to Ackergillshore with the setting sun beyond the sandy shore of Sinclair's Bay is a great way to finish a day.

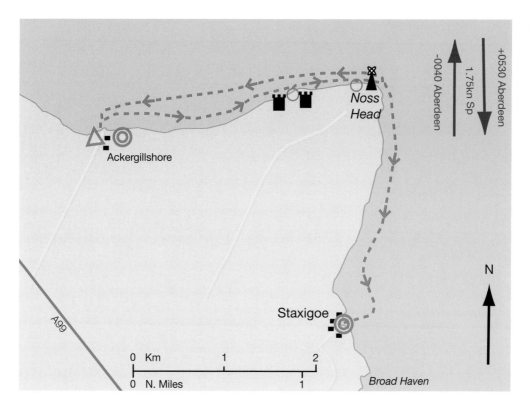

Sea stack close to the Castles

Tide & Weather

The tidal streams do not affect this bit of coast much, though you could guess that a north-going stream might create an eddy in Sinclair's Bay, which would run from Ackergillshore eastward toward Noss Head.

The cliffs provide enough shelter to paddle this trip when there is quite a strong wind blowing from the south, but going beyond the lighthouse would be a big challenge. The sea is noticeably more active to the north and east of the lighthouse, by going no further this trip can be kept quite easy.

Additional Information

This trip could quite easily be extended by going round Noss Head and down to Staxigoe, but watch out for the more active sea from the lighthouse south, see the note above.

Staxigoe to Lybster

No. 41 | Grade B | 24km | 5-6 Hours | OS Sheet 11 & 12 | Tidal Port Aberdeen

Start	△ Staxigoe (385525)
Finish	◎ Lybster Bay (244348)
HW/LW	HW at Lybster is around 2 hours before Aberdeen.
Tidal times	At the northern end of this journey, between Noss Head and Wick: The SSW going stream starts 5 hrs and 30 mins after HW Aberdeen. The NNE going stream starts about 40 mins before HW Aberdeen.
	10km south-west of the end of this trip, at Dunbeath: The SW going stream starts about 6 hrs after HW Aberdeen. The NE going stream starts about 20 mins before HW Aberdeen.
Tidal rates	Tidal streams from Wick Bay northward to around Noss Head, (389550). Here is a tidal stream that can run at about 1.75 knots on an average spring tide.
	Off Dunbeath Bay, 10km SW of Lybster, there is a bit of a tidal stream that, on average should not exceed 1 knot at springs.
Coastguard	Aberdeen, tel:01224 592334, VHF Weather 0730 UT

One of the several arches on this superb trip

Introduction

A stunning bit of east coast scenery, in fact enough to make some diehards, who say the west coast is the only place to paddle, 'eat their hats'.

With steep cliffs for the majority of the journey, many caves and huge arches, teeming with bird life in the spring and summer, and a few seals, this is a trip worth keeping for a special day. On a calm day you will be able to paddle into more of the caves, through the arches and find somewhere to land more easily.

Description

Starting at Staxigoe keeps the trip associated with a quieter experience throughout. At just over 1km, the crossing of Wick Bay will be the furthest distance that you will venture from the coast on this trip. Wick harbour plays host to a variety of commercial seagoing traffic, traditionally fishing boats but in recent times they have been joined by service and exploratory ships for the support and extension of the offshore oil production industry. Therefore keep a watchful eye open for boats coming into the harbour that might appear over your left shoulder from behind as you cross the mouth of the bay.

In less than an hour after starting to paddle you will be approaching the 'Castle of Old Wick'. The presence of Vikings in this and many other parts of Scotland is well documented, and this castle could easily have been used by Saint Rognvald, Earl of Orkney, known for his part in creating the Cathedral of St Magnus in Kirkwall, Orkney, starting in 1137. The castle itself stands on a precipitous neck of rock that has a protective ditch on the approach from the land.

From here the cliff scenery continues all the way down to Lybster and beyond. The calmer the sea the better the opportunity will be to explore the geos, caves, arches and stacks, with many of the cliffs being sheer and around 45m high. Paddling really close to their bases is a wonderful experience, especially when traversing between walls on both sides, such as in the narrow geos and under arches.

Whaligoe, (321402), is without comparison. A series of 350 flagstone steps zigzag their way down a steep cliff to a narrow geo that once was a tiny fishing harbour. This harbour was built in the 18th Century, and once saw the harvest of many barrels of herring laboriously carried up the steps by the women of Whaligoe. All that remains today of that important industry here in Whaligoe are the ruins of a house at the bottom of the steps and evidence of winding gear that very cleverly managed to pull boats inward, with the help of a pulley system attached to the back wall of the geo. Carrying the many barrels of herring up the steps must have been a backbreaking, thigh pumping experience. Visiting this hidden gem will perhaps suggest the magnitude of the lure of the herring, almost a 'gold rush' of sorts. To create a fishing station at such a difficult location must reflect the lack of easier sites along the cliff-ridden coast and a huge desire to be involved in the harvest of herring.

Don't be fooled into thinking that because Whaligoe was a fishing harbour, that it is a good place to come ashore and cut short the trip. Anything lively from the east or north-east would

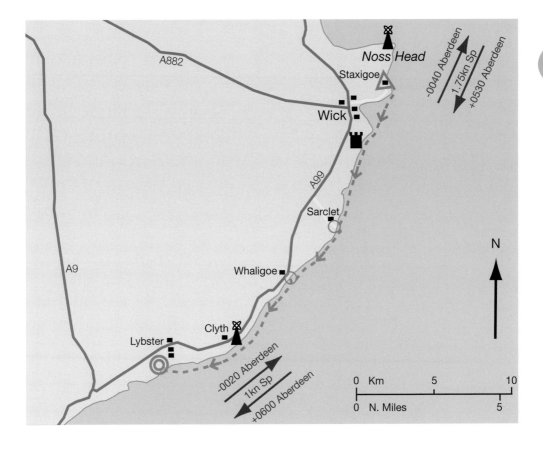

make it very difficult to safely land. If you did succeed, then the carry up the 350 steps would certainly finish you off!

The Haven, (351433), just below Sarclet, would perhaps be worthy of consideration as a possible exit, though as with the majority of the coast, any time there is a wind or swell with an easterly element, the landing will be difficult.

Within 2kms of leaving Whaligoe you will need to change from OS Sheet 12 to OS Sheet 11.

The cliff scenery continues unabated, with evidence of large important nest sites for many hundreds of seabirds that would include guillemots, razorbills and kittiwakes. Remember that if you are passing beneath these nest sites during the breeding season, that you should keep a bit further away from the cliff.

Having circumnavigated the impressive Stack of Mid Clyth you approach two important areas for rock climbing. The first, Mid Clyth, is easily located by the small lighthouse atop the cliff (290363), and the second area, Occumster, is about 1.5km before Lybster. Most of the routes were first climbed or recorded around 1990-1992. As with all climbs, they are recorded in the Scottish Mountaineering Club climbing guidebooks; refer to the ' Northern Highlands, Volume Two ', for this area. Mid Clyth is perhaps known to others for its some 200 standing stones that radiate outward in 2 separate fans. Make a point of going into the little bay (251350), about 600m before you go round the corner into Lybster Bay. Here is a smaller stack than some of the others that grace this coastline, but it does have a small through route and a fine colour to the rock, especially with a lowering sun.

Lybster harbour, its first pier constructed at the outset of the herring boom in 1810, does indeed provide a very sheltered place to enter or leave the water. If it is relatively calm you can put ashore

Sea cliff climbing

just left of all the harbour walls, on a pebble shore, then it is just a short carry up to the car, which you can park at the top of the shore.

Tide & Weather

This is just the sort of trip to do when the tidal range is greater than an average spring tide, and there is a slight breeze from the NE, but no swell to speak of. With a noticeable swell coming in from the North Sea, landing for breaks and paddling into caves will be difficult.

The bigger range translates into a faster tidal stream; add to that a pushing wind, and the 24km will seem like a cruise. Start the trip, if possible, just as the SSW going stream starts to run at 5 hours and 30 minutes after HW Aberdeen.

One of the few landing spots

More than likely, at tides less than average springs, the wind direction and strength on this journey might play a more significant part in deciding which way you do this trip.

Additional Information

The large harbour of Wick does provide an alternative launch site on the north side of the river basin at (367509) beside the public toilets and a car park, as does Broad Haven (381514).

The rifle range and the associated danger area marked on the 1:50,000, just south of Wick is used by the Territorial Army. Phone them on 01 955 603 551, or phone the Aberdeen Coastguard to check if any danger exists on the day you plan to kayak this stretch of coast.

There is a fine café within the harbour at Lybster to relax in at the end of your journey.

Fort George and Chanonry Point

No. 42 | Grade A | 12km | 3 Hours | OS Sheet 27 | Tidal Port Aberdeen

Start	△ Ardersier (780544)
Finish	◎ Ardersier (780544)
HW/LW	HW/LW at Ardersier is about 1 hr and 20 mins before Aberdeen.
Tidal times	Between Chanonry Point and Fort George: The ingoing stream starts about 6 hrs and 5 mins after HW Aberdeen. The outgoing stream starts about 1 hr and 5 mins before HW Aberdeen.
Tidal rates	The average spring rate outgoing stream flows at 3.5 knots. The average spring rate ingoing stream flows at 2.5 knots.
Coastguard	Aberdeen, tel:01224 592334, VHF Weather 0730 UT

Introduction

This is a fine short trip for an evening kayak after work. Chanonry Point is known to many locals as the place to visit if you want a good chance of seeing the resident dolphins. Fort George is an impressive fortification that is still used by the military.

Bottlenose dolphins in the Moray Firth

Description

There is a small parking area on the left of the road adjacent to a house just above the shore at (780544). The carry down to the water can be quite long if you arrive here at low water during springs, but the ground is firm sand with a bit of rock and weed, so travelling over it is not a great problem. Due to the proximity of houses, please be discreet when changing.

Fort George stands at the northern end of the large curving beach; it was built during the period 1747 to 1769 after the Jacobite risings in 1745/6. The fort has never been seriously attacked and remains in excellent condition despite being around 250 years old. It is still used by the military and the Queen's Own Highlanders museum is contained within the fort. Historic Scotland look after this magnificent property and it is open to the public throughout the year. So large is the site that in the summer months a small train transports visitors on a circular route within the grounds.

The Jacobites were those who chose to support James VII and his son James Francis Edward Stuart, and in turn his son Charles Edward Stewart, better known as 'Bonnie Prince Charlie'. In 1740 Charles wrote to his father, 'I go Sire, in search of three crowns, which I doubt not but to have the honour and happiness of laying at your majesty's feet. If I fail in the attempt, your next sight of me will be in my coffin'. At one point in his attempt to be king of Scotland, England and Ireland his army of followers had captured Edinburgh and Carlisle. One of the most notable massacres in the history of the Jacobite uprisings was at Culloden Moor, just 15km to the south west of Fort George, where many highlanders lost their lives fighting for 'Bonnie Prince Charlie' on the 16th April 1746.

Anywhere on this trip you might be lucky enough to see the bottlenose dolphins that live here all year round. Quite a large tourist industry has grown based around these mammals; special wildlife tours by boat can be taken to view the great diversity of life in the Moray Firth, with the dolphins being top of the list for things to see. The dolphins might come quite close to your kayak and they can be up to 4m in length, so nice as it is to see them, when they jump out of the water you certainly hope that they do not land on you! The dolphins have been studied for many years now and as many as 130 individuals are recognised by their characteristic features, such as notches on their fins and patterned scarring on their backs.

The dolphins share these waters with minke whales, which are often seen in the autumn, and harbour porpoises that live here all year round. The porpoises are about half the size of the dolphins with a much smaller fin on their backs, which has a more rounded top to it in comparison to the more pointed top seen on the dolphins' dorsal fin. The porpoises suffer from aggressive attacks by dolphins that throw their smaller cousins into the air and play with them as a cat does with a mouse. Kayakers have found dead porpoises with dolphin tooth marks on their flanks lying in the water and some video footage was taken a number of years ago of a dolphin tossing a porpoise like a rag doll into the air.

Over at Rosemarkie there is a fine beach, which at its north end changes into a rockier coast; this is a good spot to land for a break.

Kayaking back along the sandy shore toward Chanonry Point affords a good view across to Fort George. The sea will undoubtedly be more active at Chanonry Point, it is probably this turbulence that stirs up the marine life and attracts the dolphins in search of food.

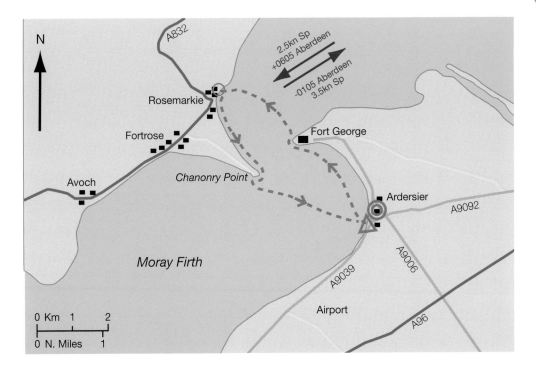

Tide & Weather

If the tidal streams are running fast, expect to experience eddies at Chanonry Point and around the headland that Fort George occupies.

The pilot would suggest that there is slack water between the following times:

From 2 hours and 20 minutes before HW Aberdeen until 1 hour and 5 minutes before HW Aberdeen, and from 4 hours and 40 minutes after HW Aberdeen until 6 hours and 5 minutes after HW Aberdeen.

Outwith these times you should expect to experience moving water which is most noticeable off the two headlands.

Additional Information

If you want to find out more about Fort George, visit Historic Scotland's website www.historic-scotland.gov.uk.

Cummingston to Covesea

No. 43 | Grade A | 10km | 3 Hours | OS Sheet 28 | Tidal Port Aberdeen

Start	△ Hopeman Harbour (145699)
Finish	◎ Hopeman Harbour (145699)
HW/LW	HW/LW at Burghead is about 1 hour and 30 minutes before Aberdeen.
Tidal times	Off Covesea: The E going stream starts about 20 mins before HW Aberdeen. The W going stream starts about 5 hrs and 45 mins after HW Aberdeen.
Tidal rates	The average spring rate out at the above point is 0.5 knots.
Coastguard	Aberdeen, tel:01224 592334, VHF Weather 0730 UT

Introduction

Save this trip for a sunny evening so that the sun will be shining on the superbly coloured sandstone cliffs. Kittiwakes, cormorants, shags, fulmars and terns all use this bit of coastline as do rock climbers and fishermen.

Part of the coast is a SSSI (Site of Special Scientific Interest), due to the dinosaur footprints that can be found in the bedding planes of the sandstone.

Description

The harbour has 2 sections, the east part is most convenient for launching your kayak in.

Head out to the west passing the west beach, backed by the caravan site of Hopeman and soon you will be alongside the popular rock climbing cliffs of Cummingston. There is a wide low-roofed cave that you can paddle into at high water and on the roof you will see slings that have been used by climbers in an attempt to traverse the roof of the cave. A little further on is the main climbing area with most of the climbs on the north-facing walls, but there are also climbs on the sea stacks.

Return eastward past the harbour and you will notice all the brightly coloured beach huts up behind the yellow sand of the east beach. Clashach Cove is a good place to stop for a rest and explore. Before landing, if the tide is right you might be able to kayak through the natural arch on the right of the bay. The easiest time to land in Clashach Cove is at low tide when there will be sand to land on. Above this it becomes a mixture of rock and sand, finally grading into a steeper stony beach if you land during periods of high water. Until you land, you will not be able to see the land cave tucked in at the back left-hand corner at the base of the yellow cliff. This cave has been above the level of the sea for many years and it is said that it was used as a dwelling right up until the 1960's. Close by there is a small tunnel-like arch that you can walk through for a view over the sea to the north. Further along the coast at Covesea there are more caves that were lived in by families up until recent times; photographic evidence of these modern cave dwellers exists in historical accounts of this area.

The natural coastline beyond Clashach Cove has been covered by the spoil from the quarry behind; it was in this quarry and others along this coast that the dinosaur footprints were found.

The desirability of using this natural stone for building can be seen from the fine display of colours shown in the cliffs; yellow, orange and reds that deepen in colour as the evening light comes round onto the cliffs sell this rock. The quarry lay unused for many years but recently it was re-opened to provide high quality stone to clad the extension to the National Museum of Scotland in Edinburgh.

Kittiwakes nest on the steeper parts of the cliffs, their nesting sites are easy to see from the distance because of the ice white streaks that mark the rocks below their nests.

Before you reach the Covesea lookout tower a rising line of dry caves can be seen above the beach. One of them is known as the 'Sculptors Cave', and has Pictish drawings on its walls. Burghead, the town 4km to the west of Hopeman is known as the 'Pictish Capital' and it has a visitor centre where you can find out more about the Picts.

Slightly further to the east from the lookout tower there is a two-legged sea stack with a relatively easy landing just in front of it. If you go round the back of the stack you will see where the egg hunters of years gone by have cut out handholds and foot holes in the form of pigeon-hole steps up the initial steep part of the east leg.

From here the return journey into the setting sun awaits, with the hope that if you haven't seen the dolphins yet, you might on the way home.

Tide & Weather

There is very little in the way of noticeable tidal stream activity along this stretch of coast, so it is not unreasonable to venture out at any state of the tide.

If the wind does pick up, the sea around the harbour walls including the entrance can become quite confused with clapotis. Landing at Clashach Cove could be difficult when there is a swell running, producing a bit of surf.

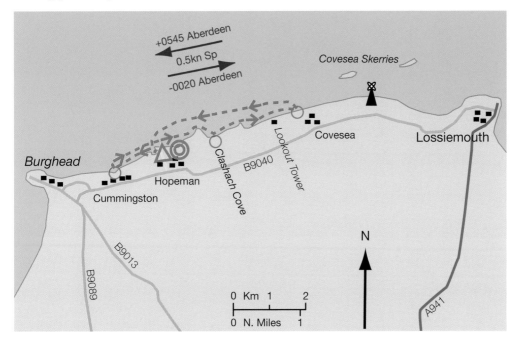

43

Climbers on 'Centre' a Mild VS 4b at Cummingston

Additional Information

At the entrance to Clashach Quarry there are some interpretive noticeboards providing information about the dinosaur footprints that have been found along this stretch of the coast.

If you do need rescuing after falling into the sea, this is the place to do it. The RAF Search and Rescue helicopters are based only a few kilometres to the east at RAF Lossiemouth!

Cliffs before Downie Bay

Troup Head

No. 44 | Grade B | 12km | 3 Hours | OS Sheet 30 | Tidal Port Aberdeen

Start	△ Aberdour Bay (886646)
Finish	◎ Gardenstown (799648)
HW/LW	HW/LW at Gardenstown is about 1 hour and 10 minutes before Aberdeen.
Tidal times	The E going stream starts about 3 hrs and 50 mins before HW Aberdeen. The W going stream starts about 2 hrs and 10 mins after HW Aberdeen.
Tidal rates	The average spring rate is between 0.5 and 0.75 of a knot along the coast. Off Troup Head it flows a bit faster, at around 1.5 to 2 knots.
Coastguard	Aberdeen, tel:01224 592334, VHF Weather 0730 UT

Introduction

This stretch of cliffy coastline supports many thousands of breeding seabirds including the only mainland breeding site for gannets; hence this area has been designated as a Special Protection Area as well as a SSSI (Site of Special Scientific Interest).

Pennan Harbour

The cliffs are up to 100m in height with caves and skerries at their feet, where seals haul out and bask in the sunshine. The villages are picturesque with small harbours and colourful houses.

Description

There is a marked contrast between the rich red sandstone cliffs, with obvious caves to the east of the stony beach and the grey metamorphic rock to the west that lead onto Troup Head.

It was here in 1884 that Jane Whyte, a local lady, saved the lives of 15 men whose ship had lost power in a storm whilst passing Troup Head. The ship drifted at the mercy of the sea and the storm until it reached Aberdour Bay. The crew were clinging onto their sinking ship when they saw Jane come to the beach. They threw her a rope, she swam out through the surf and confused waves to reach the rope which she took ashore and one by one all of the crew were saved, thanks to her heroic efforts. In due course Jane's bravery was to be recognised and she received the RNLI's Silver Medal.

Even without a storm raging, Aberdour Bay can have dumpy surf through which setting off could prove to be a wet experience. To avoid this, you can go over the little burn to the west of the car park and put in amongst the channels between the skerries that stretch out to sea and dampen down the waves.

Not long after leaving the bay the cliffs start to rise up. The interesting rock architecture that this trip is known for starts with a large arch, which you can paddle under, but usually have to return the same way.

At Strahangles Point the rock becomes more interesting once more as it changes to conglomerate. The cliffs are steep and grassy reaching up to 100m and more, and have an unusual feel for the east coast. It is the sort of scenery you might expect to come across on the islands of Skye or Mull. In the bays beyond go in as close as you can to the shore to gain the full effect of the high cliffs, which have arches and skerries at their feet. Many grey seals play in around this area, some have resting spots inside caves and come rushing out as you pass the entrances, but the majority of them are found relaxing on the many skerries. The village of Pennan appeared on the map for most people in 1983 when it was chosen as a filming location for 'Local Hero' a film about an American oil company that wants to buy a Scottish village so it can replace it with an oil refinery. The telephone box in the film was a focal point for calls between America and Scotland; despite the real telephone box not being the one used in the film it draws many film buffs/tourists each year. The harbour provides a good spot to land and have a bite to eat; if you have forgotten your sandwiches, do not despair, the Pennan Inn can provide you with all you need. Pennan was known for more traditional reasons, as it was a producer of millstones as well as being a fishing village. The houses are squeezed between the shore and the steep ground behind them, with their gable ends placed to face the ravages of the sea.

The cliffs after Pennan become more vertical and attractive to nesting birds. Along this coast in 1995 there were: kittiwake – 31,000 pairs, guillemot – 44,600 pairs, fulmar – 4,400 pairs, all nesting along with numerous shags, herring gulls, razorbills, puffins and gannets.

Just before you pass 'Lion's Head' look up onto the grassy slope above the cliff and you will see a hole-like scar on the hillside, this is the mouth of a blowhole refered to as 'Hell's Lum' on the map. If you look closely at the map, the subterranean tunnel that connects the sea entrance to the top of the chimney is marked as 2 dashed lines. Once past Lion's Head go close in and look backwards for the narrow slot that is illuminated within by a shaft of light coming down the blowhole.

About 540 pairs of gannets nest on the cliffs at Troup Head, the only mainland colony in Scotland. When you kayak past there will be a sky full of gannets above you and still yet more of

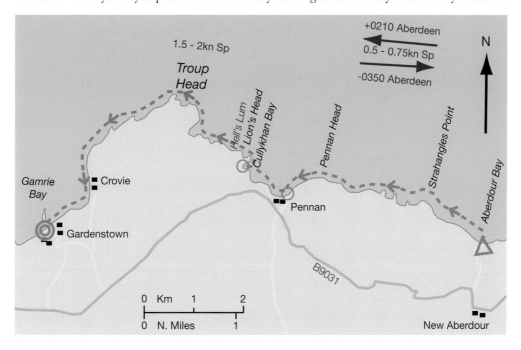

Herring gulls guarding their stack

them sitting peacefully on their nests made of all things including colourful ropes discarded or lost by fishermen. Sometimes the sea can be a bit jumpy here and trying to get a photograph of the gannets requires the stability of another kayaker coming alongside.

The route continues, passing some fine sea stacks where there are often puffins below, casually paddling in the water. The next village is Crovie and it was established when families were cleared from the inland farms and estates in the latter part of the 18th Century to make way for sheep. Clearances such as these are more often associated with the highlands and islands of Scotland. Crovie has changed little over the years, due in part to the restricted site where the village is, so tight are the houses against the cliffs that there is no road in the village. Fishing was the only way for the displaced families to make a living, they had no land to cultivate or graze sheep and cattle on. Fishing from Crovie as an industry came to a sharp end when a storm in January 1953 destroyed the footpath to Gardenstown and also washed away some houses and sheds.

Gardenstown used to be called Gamrie, as it is still refered to by many locals. It is the largest of the 3 villages on this trip and has grown significantly over the years. Down at the harbour the old houses are crammed in just like the previous 2 villages, but high up on the hillside there are new houses which contrast significantly with the fisher houses in Seatown to the west of the harbour. If you take a walk along the sands to the west of the last houses you will see the cliffs are made of a lovely sandstone with swirls of red and white and in places, some unusual circular spots of creamy white sandstone.

Tide & Weather

Try to arrive at Troup Head in the last hour of the west-going stream, this can be achieved by leaving Pennan harbour after a break, at about 5 hours before HW Aberdeen.

Fulmar

44

The fulmar is a seabird that has recently colonised much new territory. Originally St Kilda (60km to the west of North Uist in the Outer Hebrides) was the only place in the British Isles where the fulmar lived, but since the late 1800's it has become a common sight around the Scottish coast. If you visit the Monach Isles, Trip 29, you might be lucky enough to see St Kilda in the distance to the NW. On the Monach Isles there are no cliffs for the fulmar to nest on as it usually prefers, so the adaptable fulmar nests on the ground. If you go too close to a fulmar on its nest, whether climbing or walking, the bird is unlikely to fly away. Instead it makes sure you, as the unwelcome intruder, leave with a very unpleasant oily substance that really stinks, all over your face. It was this oil that the inhabitants of St Kilda harvested to fuel lamps thereby enabling them to illuminate the dark interiors of their blackhouses. Of all the birds that you will see paddling around the Scottish coast, none are more inquisitive than the fulmar. Many times the birds will fly past at close quarters for a look, gracefully sweeping in from above, cruising down to almost clip the surface of the water and then rise to sweep past you at eye level. Who's watching who?

The very high grassy cliffs between Aberdour Bay and Pennan can provide shelter if a strong southerly wind is blowing, but equally they can produce strong downdraughts at the same time.

Gannets

Additional Information

There is a good café in the harbour area of Gardenstown. The villagers maintain the harbour and there is an honesty box, which all users of the harbour are encouraged to leave a donation in.

If you can wait until a sunny summer's evening to do this trip, then consider travelling from Gardenstown to Aberdour Bay. The low evening light that will shine on the cliffs is absolutely fantastic.

Cruden Bay

No. 45 | **Grade B** | **10km** | **3 Hours** | **OS Sheet 30** | **Tidal Port Aberdeen**

Start	△ Port Erroll (Cruden Bay) (094356)
Finish	◎ Boddam Harbour (134426)
HW/LW	HW/LW at Cruden Bay is about the same time as Aberdeen.
Tidal times	In general, along this part of the coast; The NNE going stream starts around HW Aberdeen. The SSW going stream starts around LW Aberdeen.
Tidal rates	The average spring rate is 1.75 knots in both directions.
Coastguard	Aberdeen, tel: 01224 592334, VHF Weather 0730 UT

Introduction

This a gem of a trip along an impressive coastline dominated by granite cliffs. For many years rock climbers have used the cliffs for sport, but for an even longer time thousands of seabirds have made these cliffs home during their breeding season. Despite the hardness of the rock, the relentless work of the waves has produced several caves and a fine selection of natural arches. The Skerry just north of Boddam should not be missed; this little rock usually has many of our larger seals, the Atlantic grey, relaxing, spread out all over the rock.

Description

At the north end of the Bay of Cruden is a fine little harbour noted on the map as Port Erroll. Within the harbour, very close to the parking, there is a slipway with a clean sandy beach next to it, which makes for an easy and pleasant start to the day.

Shortly after leaving the harbour, the rock scenery starts with some small skerries that you can weave in and out of. After 1.5 km the ruin of Slains Castle dominates the skyline. Some would say that it was this castle that provided Bram Stoker with the inspiration to write his famous novel 'Dracula'. Whatever, this castle is an imposing sight from the sea, huge gaping holes in the walls where the large windows once faced the full rage of storms coming in from the North Sea and perched on the very edge of the cliffs. The full size and grandeur of this castle is best appreciated by making a visit to the castle from the landward side.

The first of the several arches housed by this coast is just around the corner, called the Bow, a double arch. Alas, this arch is passed through not by kayak but on foot as it sits high above the sea.

Passing the Twa Havens, pronounced as in the French word 'trois' for three, but meaning Two Havens, you will see the island of Dunbuy ahead, smothered in seabirds. This too has an arch up in the sky. As you approach the guillemots will be constantly streaming off the cliff heading out to sea. Going through the channel between Dunbuy and the mainland you will see the kittiwakes' nests on the mainland cliff.

On the way up to the Bullers of Buchan be sure to search out the natural arch going through the long promontory just round the corner north of Path-head. The Bullers of Buchan is a popular tourist attraction, so don't be surprised to see people looking down at you as you come through the large entrance arch into the 'Boiler of Buchan', a place of calm if you venture in with your kayak, but a ferocious place when a large sea is crashing in from the east.

North Haven presents an opportunity to get out and stretch the legs, though as with the other potential landing spots, it is likely to be a bouldery rather than a sandy experience. The little subsidiary bay on the left has an interesting small natural arch, which you can pass through just before landing.

Referring to the 'North East Outcrops', the guidebook used by rock climbers for this area, you will find, 'Walrus Ridge', 'Alligator Ridge', 'Bridal Cave' and 'Bloody Hole' on the next section of coast up to Murdoch Head. Much of this area has been quarried in the past for the good quality granite, collectively known as the Longhaven Quarries, most of which are before Yoags' Haven. Just past Murdoch Head is the Round Tower, sitting high up on the left. It is an impressive tower with one of the finest concentrations of hard rock climbs on the coast.

Hare Craig and the other islands in Long Haven are favoured nesting sites for the birds, being inaccessible for land-based predators. Be sure to give the nesting birds a wide berth to avoid too much disturbance. Beyond Long Haven there are numerous nooks and crannies to explore, the occasional rock climber might be seen, as there are fewer birds on some of the walls.

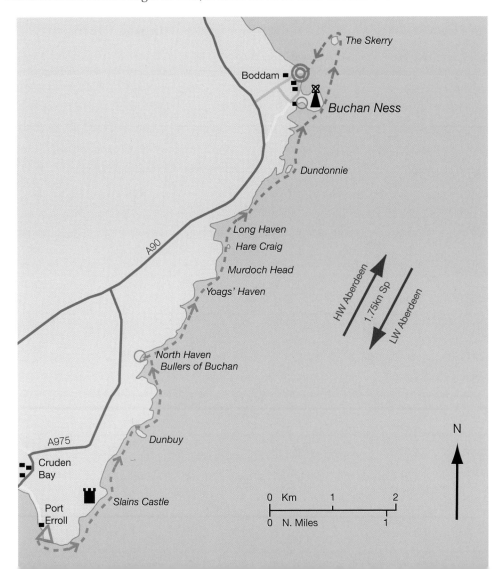

Buchan Ness lighthouse

The Buchan Ness lighthouse which stands on an island connected to the mainland by a bridge, was built in 1827. The distinctive red bands on the tower were added in 1907 as an aid to identifying it more easily during the day. During the Second World War a mine washed ashore here and exploded; fortunately no one was killed or injured but the lighthouse and the out buildings were damaged, broken windows, slates of the roof and broken doors being the worst of the damage. As with other lighthouses the light has been improved over the years from an initial 6,500 candlepower to 2,000,000 candlepower, giving a range of 28 nautical miles. At high water it is a short carry from the south bay to the north bay across the ridge of stones under the bridge. If you look closely in the stones you will find pieces of flint, which do not occur naturally on this coast of granite rocks, the explanation is that they would have been originally used as ballast on ships and then thrown overboard when the ship took on its cargo.

The Skerry, about 1 kilometre NNE from the lighthouse is a rock that can be smothered in large grey seals. Definitely take the time to kayak out to this skerry, it is a lively place once the seals start swimming around you.

Return, passing Meikle Mackie to enter Boddam harbour and land in the far right corner.

Tide & Weather

If you choose to do this trip and return to Port Erroll the same way, leave Port Erroll 3 hours after HW Aberdeen, so the start of the return journey will coincide with the start of the SSW going stream at LW Aberdeen. Fortunately due to the nature of the coast there are opportunities to eddy hop on the way back if timings don't work out so well.

Inverbervie to Stonehaven

No. 46 | Grade B | 15km | 4 Hours | OS Sheet 45 | Tidal Port Aberdeen

Start	△ Inverbervie (833721)
Finish	◎ Stonehaven (877854)
HW/LW	HW/LW at Stonehaven is about 10 minutes after Aberdeen.
Tidal times	At a point 6 nautical miles off Stonehaven:
	The SSW going stream starts about 4 hours before HW Aberdeen.
	The NNE going stream starts about 2 hours after HW Aberdeen.
Tidal rates	The average spring rate at the above point is about 1.75 knots.
Coastguard	Forth, tel:01333 450666, VHF Weather 0730 UT

Introduction

This section of the Scottish east coast is a haven for breeding birds. The conglomerate cliffs are steep and inaccessible to most predators, so the birds can nest in their thousands. Many skerries, inlets, caves and the sheer cliffs make this an interesting trip, best seen in the early morning light when the sun enhances the colours of the rock and the colourful lichens that grow over the rocks.

Todhead lighthouse

Description

Inverbervie is the sort of village that most people would just keep driving through unless they had heard about the award winning fish and chip shop! But Inverbervie has a better claim to fame, it was where Hercules Linton, the designer of the famous 'Cutty Sark' was born. The Cutty Sark was designed to be fast, a sailing ship that could hopefully be the fastest back from China with the first cargo of the new season's tea. In this she failed but later in life she was several times the fastest ship from Australia to Britain. Inverbervie was a mill town that for almost 200 years spun flax in a number of mills along the River Bervie; it was the first village in Scotland to open a flax-spinning mill in 1790.

As soon as you leave Bervie Bay the coastline comes alive, the rocky coast with its skerries and small islets are busy with birds. Up above Crooked Haven is the old church of Kinneff; it was here that the Scottish crown jewels were hidden under the clay floor. The crown jewels had been moved to Dunnottar Castle further up the coast for safe keeping, but the English army under the command of Oliver Cromwell lay siege to the castle. Prior to the castle succumbing to the strength of the English army, the Scottish crown jewels were successfully smuggled out and taken to Kinneff Church where they lay for 9 years before being returned to Edinburgh Castle.

Todhead lighthouse, a typical white tower was built in 1897, showing a feeble 42,500 candlepower light; it now shines at 3 million candlepower reaching out for 18 miles into the North Sea.

Catterline, a small village with a long association with fishing is now more associated with art. There are several well-known artists living in Catterline who get inspiration from the contrasting weather, calm and peaceful in the summer months but a wild place at the height of a January storm coming in from the east. During the First World War a German U-boat was able to capture

5 fishermen who were line fishing off Catterline, their boat the 'Bella' was blown up and they remained prisoners until the end of the war.

The Garran, about one kilometre north of Catterline, is a fantastic hidden bay accessed through a wide arch. It might be possible with a really high tide to get out over the rock bar to the north of the bay, otherwise you come in and go out the same way.

Up to this point you will have seen many birds but from Crawton northward for 3 kilometres you will see thousands of birds. The numbers of birds quoted for here during the breeding season is a staggering 170,000. It is little wonder that this section of coast known as Fowlsheugh is a RSPB bird reserve. Keeping a couple of hundred metres off from the cliffs to afford the nesting birds a bit of space doesn't lessen the experience. The air is full of birds, great waves of guillemots pass overhead. The sea is peppered with birds as well, many of them puffins. The cliffs are made of conglomerate, which could be described as nature's concrete, but for its more interesting colours

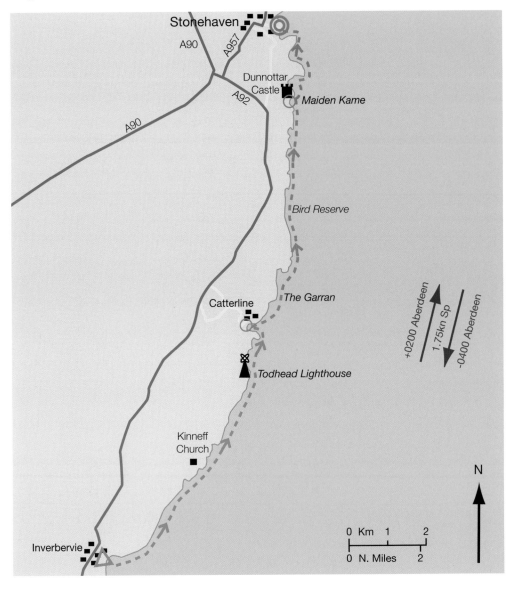

46

and variety of stones between the cement. As the cliff weathers, rounded rocks fall out of the cliff leaving a hemispherical space behind. These isolated holes of many sizes make great nesting sites for the birds, small ones occupied by single pairs with larger holes being occupied by several breeding pairs, most commonly guillemots.

Up at the Maiden Kame seek out the long slender passage under an arch that you can paddle through to find yourself in another inlet by which you can go back out to sea.

Dunnottar Castle sits on an isolated rock 50m high, only connected to the mainland by a narrow ridge. This rock was an ideal place to build a castle, as it is very easy to defend if only attacked by foot soldiers. When cannons came on the scene it was possible to damage the structure as well as starve the occupants by making sure no supplies went into the castle. Oliver Cromwell's siege with artillery lasted 8 months in 1651 before the occupants surrendered, but not before the Scottish crown jewels had successfully been smuggled away. In 1990 Dunnottar Castle was used as a location to film a version of 'Hamlet' starring Mel Gibson.

The final part of the journey is as interesting as the rest. Take the time to hug the coastline on this last section before going into the harbour and landing in the far right-hand corner on clean sand beside the slipway, right outside the pub!

Tide & Weather

Tidal stream information for this area is scant, therefore if you do come across a stream of water going against you it might be possible to use the indented coastline to eddy hop, or indeed if it is eddies that you are punching against, consider going further out.

A swell coming in off the North Sea would make starting at Inverbervie difficult, but if you wanted to get some of the trip done, go up to Catterline and launch in the shelter of the harbour.

Will the residents afford him a 'clean' passage?

Having said that, a significant swell could make the journey close to the cliffs uncomfortable, so it might be better to wait for another day.

Additional Information

To get to the put-in point follow the signs off the main street in Inverbervie down to the caravan park, to the right of this there is a car park in front of the stony beach. Drive right through this and continue along the dirt track until a grassy lay-by is found just before the green control box (Water Board) opposite the last house. From the green control box it is an easy carry down to the water, where you can put in next to the concrete covered pipe.

Isle of May

No. 47 | **Grade B** | **22km** | **6 Hours** | **OS Sheet 59** | **Tidal Port Leith**

Start	△ Anstruther Easter (568033)
Finish	◎ Anstruther Easter (568033)
HW/LW	HW/LW at Anstruther Easter is about 10 minutes before Leith.
Tidal times	At a point 3.5 nautical miles west of the Isle of May:
	The NE going stream starts about 1 hr after HW Leith.
	The SW going stream starts about 5 hrs before HW Leith.
Tidal rates	The average spring rate at the above point is about 1 knot.
Coastguard	Forth, tel:01333 450666, VHF Weather 0730 UT

Introduction

The Isle of May, known as the 'Jewel of the Forth', is a National Nature Reserve. Over 200,000 seabirds come here to breed every year, with puffins being the most numerous. The west coast is made of cliffs that rise vertically out of the sea, with caves at their base. These cliffs are where guillemots and kittiwakes nest so densely that the black rock is painted white with the droppings of thousands of birds. During the breeding season for Atlantic grey seals there will be around

3,000 seals on the island, making this the most important breeding ground for grey seals on the east coast of Scotland. This is a superb island to visit.

Description

At the harbour there is a car park, just to the east of the Lifeboat Station, that is right at the top of the sandy beach enclosed within the harbour. Anstruther Easter has long been an important port with ships sailing to the Mediterranean for wine and the Baltic regions for timber. During the heyday of herring fishing there was a large fleet based here, and today in the village you can visit the Scottish Fisheries Museum to discover more about the history of Anstruther.

The journey out to the Isle of May will not be a lonely one if you visit the island in early summer. Shortly after setting out you are likely to have puffins as companions, bobbing about on the sea in small groups, becoming more numerous as you get closer to the island.

For a kayaker there are more options for landing than are available to visitors coming over by boat, though from the warden's perspective it is probably better that you land in Kirkhaven at the south-east end of the island. This bay has a few skerries at its entrance and with a swell coming in from the east, it might not be that clear how to enter. Take your time and approach from the south-east. If this is still too daunting try landing in East Tarbet or on the west coast at the north end of the island. The warden prefers to meet everyone who comes ashore, so he can provide visitors with information that helps to make your visit more interesting and also to protect the wildlife from accidental disturbance. The island has a system of marked paths, on which you should remain. A path will take you from the landing spot in Kirkhaven up to the small visitor centre and toilet; here you can pick up a leaflet illustrating the path network and telling you all about the island.

Puffins will be all around, they nest in shallow burrows (42,000 are occupied) all over the island. This in part is why you must stay on the path, as it is easy to squash a burrow which might have a bird and an egg inside. As well as the puffins, look out for 3 species of gull, 2 species of tern, eider ducks, shags and fulmars.

The second most common bird on the island is the guillemot with a tally of around 26,000 individuals. Guillemots nest on the western cliffs, which they share with up to 6,000 pairs of kittiwakes and 4,000 razorbills. It is a fantastic experience to kayak along the west side of the island surrounded by so many birds, but be careful not to go too close in to the cliff as the birds might take fright and in the process of leaving their ledges the eggs could be knocked off the cliff.

The Isle of May was the first place in Scotland to have a manned lighthouse; in the 17th Century it was nothing more than a platform on which one ton of coal was shovelled each night. If it got windy and rainy the light became difficult to see, and in storms when it was needed most, there was potentially no light to be seen. A more reliable automatic light has superceded it.

During the First World War the island was used as a signalling station to pass warnings of approaching enemy ships that might try to sail up the River Forth; an improvement on visual observation was made in the 1930's when a cable was laid from the mainland out to the island. When ships passed over this cable, changes in magnetic field could be identified, so an enemy ship trying to sneak up the Forth under the cover of darkness could be identified and the necessary action taken.

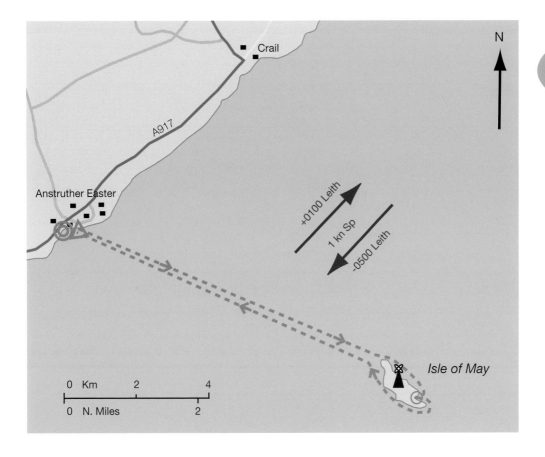

Tide & Weather

The tidal streams do not flow that fast, so you should have little trouble doing the crossing. At the NW and SE ends of the island expect to feel a bit more movement in the water as it pushes past these prominent points.

With a wind from the west, the clapotis at the base of the cliffs on the west side of the island can make journeying close in uncomfortable. A swell coming in from the east can produce enough surf to make the landings on the east coast a bit more challenging.

Additional Information

An alternative start for this trip is to set off from the caravan and camping site in Crail, (621078).

Scottish Natural Heritage produce a leaflet describing the wildlife and charting its history, which you can pick up at the visitor centre on the island or by contacting SNH via their website www.snh.org.uk.

The Scottish Fisheries Museum website can be found at www.scottish-fisheries-museum.org.

The Scottish Seabird Centre in North Berwick has a web cam positioned on the Isle of May; visit their website www.seabird.org for lots of information about seabirds as well as a glimpse of the Isle of May.

Firth of Forth

No. 48 | **Grade A** | **20km** | **5 Hours** | **OS Sheet 65 & 66** | **Tidal Port Leith**

Start	△ South Queensferry (136784)
Finish	◎ South Queensferry (136784)
HW/LW	HW/LW at Cramond Island is the same as Leith.
Tidal times	Between the Forth Bridges:
	The E going stream starts about 30 minutes after HW Leith.
	The W going stream starts about 5 hrs and 30 mins before HW Leith.
	Beyond Oxcars:
	The W going stream starts about 5 hrs and 55 mins before HW Leith.
	The E going stream starts about HW Leith.
Tidal rates	There are three areas on this trip where the tidal streams run at their fastest:
	Under the Forth bridges the average spring rate can reach 4.5 knots.
	In Mortimer's Deep the average spring rate can reach 2.5 knots.
	Between Oxcars and Inchcolm the average spring rate can reach 3 knots.
Coastguard	Forth, tel:01333 450666, VHF Weather 0730 UT

St Colms Abbey, Inchcolm

Introduction

Launching your sea kayak and looking up to the Forth Rail Bridge is an incredible experience, and definitely the best view possible of this historical monument. Once afloat you will have started a journey that will take you to islands that are rich in history, support a surprising amount of wildlife, and have some strong tidal streams. All this provides a unique paddling experience with Edinburgh City and its Castle as the backdrop. The seals and porpoises enjoy the Forth, as do many kayakers.

Description

The launch site under the Forth Rail Bridge is shared with the Inchcolm Ferry, which is well signposted from the main roads. This gives plenty of parking and stunning views of both the road and rail bridges. This is also the site of the historical Hawes Inn that can provide a welcome refreshment at the end of the journey. On leaving the launch site, head out under the rail bridge to the first island of the day, Inch Garvie.

When kayaking under the rail bridge try to pick a section where there is no work being carried out overhead. There is often a rescue boat positioned under the bridge for the workers. This is very different from what it was like for the 4000 workers during the seven years it took to build the bridge, starting in 1882. In this period 57 died and over 500 were injured, this being considered very good safety at the time. When asked about these accidents the bridge engineer Sir Benjamin Baker is reputed to have said, 'Many would have escaped had it not been for the whisky of the Hawes Inn'. The Forth Rail Bridge opened in 1890 as the largest cantilever bridge in the world.

Being the largest does have its drawbacks though, as any painter involved in the ongoing task of painting the bridge will testify, it takes a long time to coat the bridge with 7000 gallons of paint!

Arriving at Inch Garvie the remains of the fortified defences are easily seen, these being maintained during the Second World War to defend the bridge. Earlier fortifications on Inch Garvie were also said to have repelled an attack by Cromwell. Over the years these same fortifications have been used as a state prison as well as a quarantine hospital for those with infectious diseases. Leaving Inch Garvie head past the tanker berth and on towards Inchcolm. This area is regularly used for large shipping, so keep an eye out for these ships and keep outside the main buoyage for additional peace of mind. Whilst paddling out to Inchcolm keep a look out for porpoises and whales that, surprisingly enough, have all been seen in this area. A sperm whale beached in the Firth of Forth during 1997, it was named 'Moby'. As with many other whales it ended up in the National Museum of Scotland Granton Research Centre, near Edinburgh. This large collection of whale specimens is only open to the public for viewing by appointment.

On arriving at Inchcolm, if grey seals have not been seen, there should be plenty of the common seals around. The sandy bays on the north side of the island give the most sheltered landing, as well as great views of St Colm's Abbey found on the island. It is well worth spending the time to explore Inchcolm that is justifiably known as the 'Iona of the East'. The island was named after St Columba who visited it in 567, and Alexander 1 founded the Abbey in 1123. The Abbey today is still remarkably well preserved and is a fantastic place to explore. In the summer months there are boat trips out to the island and a custodian lives there managing the Abbey and shop. If visiting the island during these months and making use of the island's facilities, a fee which goes towards

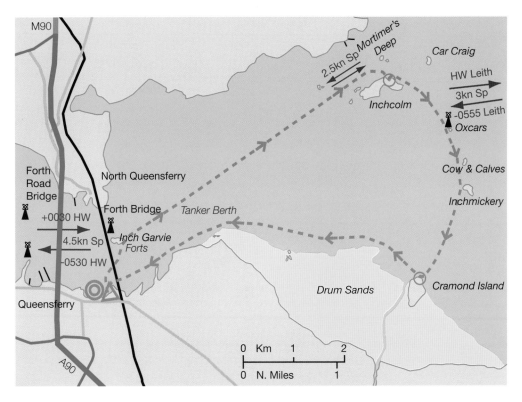

the maintenance of the Abbey is asked for by Historic Scotland. The island has also been a site of many battles over the years, due to its strategic position in the Firth of Forth and because of the riches that the Abbey held. In the 10th Century Macbeth defeated invaders and for a large price of gold allowed the invaders to bury their dead on the island. Today you can see the remains of more modern fortifications as with the other islands in the Firth, and like Inch Garvie these were also used as state prisons.

Leaving the history and wildlife of Inchcolm, look left and right before crossing the main shipping lane past Oxcars light and on to Inchmickery. The remnants of the Second World War fortification can be clearly seen here. These were said to have been built to look like the outline of a warship at anchor, and earns Inchmickery its nickname 'Battleship Island'. On from Inchmickery is the last island of the day, Cramond Island, which can be reached from the mainland at low water. This island has less history than the other islands of the day, but may offer a useful place to stretch the legs before the final section of the journey. The paddle up the Forth back to the starting point will soon pass. With the views of Edinburgh and the castle on the left, Inchcolm Abbey on the right and the ever-dominant Forth Rail and Road Bridges ahead, it is a great setting to finish a day out. All that is left are the refreshments waiting for you in the Hawes Inn; watch out for the whisky Sir Benjamin Baker warned about!

Tide & Weather

The tidal streams in this area are very strong, and even on a small neap tide they are still noticeable. If there is any wind against the tide this area can produce very rough water, which can come as a surprise considering its relatively sheltered location and close proximity to an urban landscape.

The most efficient way, and on a spring tide the only way, to kayak this trip is to go out to Inchcolm on the E going stream, which starts about 30 minutes after HW Leith. Then return from Inchmickery on the W going stream, which starts about 5 hours and 55 minutes before HW Leith. This is done by leaving South Queensferry at about 4 hours and 30 minutes after HW Leith, which should give plenty of time to enjoy the islands and have the tidal streams whisking you along in both directions.

Additional Information

An alternative start and finish from North Queensferry is also possible, starting at (122803). This will save crossing the Forth Road Toll Bridge if you are coming from the north, (80p in 2004). If you would like further information about visiting Inchcolm Island contact Historic Scotland www.historic-scotland.gov.uk who manage the island on 01383 823332.

Bass Rock

No. 49 | **Grade B** | **14km** | **4 Hours** | **OS Sheets 66 & 67** | **Tidal Port Leith**

Start	△ North Berwick (553854)
Finish	◎ North Berwick (553854)
HW/LW	HW/LW at North Berwick is about the same time as Leith.
Tidal times	At a point 3 nautical miles north-east of Bass Rock: The E going stream starts about the same time as HW Leith. The W going stream starts about 6 hrs before HW Leith.
Tidal rates	At the point noted above the average spring rate is about 0.75 knots.
Coastguard	Forth, tel:01333 450666, VHF Weather 0730 UT

Introduction

Bass Rock is home to one of the biggest gannet colonies in Scotland; as many as 40,000 pairs of gannets come here every year and virtually smother the rock so it appears white from the distance. The Latin name for gannet is 'Sula Bassana', which indicates the importance of Bass Rock as so significant the bird is named after it. This is a trip you won't forget, the noise, and the smell, the

sheer numbers of birds in the air, on the rock and on the sea. All remain indelibly etched in your mind, so when you close your eyes years after, the image is as clear as it was on the day.

Description

This impressive rock of near vertical walls on all sides is all that remains of an ancient volcano. It is the plug that formed in the centre, being made of harder rock, that has remained whilst the softer rocks around it have been worn away by the many processes of erosion, most notably glaciation. From certain angles Ailsa Craig on the west coast, can look similar to the Bass Rock, but unlike Ailsa Craig this island does not have a tame side and it is alive with birds all the way round, a full circle of activity.

The island has seen many uses over the years and it has had religious connections for a long time. The chapel was built around 1491 and is named in memory of St Baldred, an Irish missionary who it is reckoned might have been the first inhabitant as far back as the 6th Century. Since then it has often served as a prison, at one time keeping political and religious prisoners in a dungeon where many of them died. Up until around the First World War the rock was used to graze sheep, collect eggs and harvest young gannets, known as guga. The practice of killing and eating young gannets is no longer done here, but on the Hebridean Island of Lewis the locals travel once a year out to a remote island, Sula Sgeir, to harvest the guga as they have done for many years.

A good way to approach the island is to kayak eastward along the coast past the skerries called the Leithies and carry on beyond Tantallon Castle to the sandy beach due south of Bass Rock. By this time it might be worth taking a break before heading out to the rock, remember there is no landing opportunity on Bass Rock itself. Tantallon Castle is of great antiquity originally built in the 14th Century. This impregnable fortress could only be won over by using siege tactics as it stands, like Dunnottar Castle further north, on a prominent piece of ground with cliffs protecting it on three sides. Sir Walter Scott wrote the following about Tantallon:

> *Broad, massive, high and stretching far,*
> *And held impregnable in war,*
> *On a projecting rock they rose,*
> *And round three sides the ocean flows.*
> *The fourth did battled walls enclose.*

Kayaking across to the rock, the closer you get the more the sky above you will be filled with gannets circling around, as if curious to find out what you are doing. From high in the sky these birds dive down into the sea, closing their wings just before impact. Once under the water they can swim to secure a meal if a direct hit was not successful. As you pass along the base of the cliff the gannets sitting on their nests just look at you, unperturbed and confident as you drift by. The rock is not riddled with caves, but there is one superb cave that provides passage from one side of the island to the other at the correct state of the tide.

In amongst the overwhelming number of gannets, there are also puffins, guillemots and razorbills, many of which float about in rafts on the sea all around your kayak.

Travel back the same way, stopping at another sandy beach, Canty Bay for a change of scene, or go directly to the island of Craigleith and then back into North Berwick.

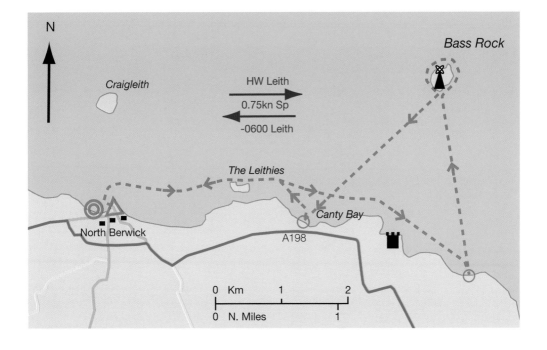

Gannets in flight

Nesting gannets

Gannet on a rock

Gannets

Gannets are one of the largest European seabirds and some of the biggest breeding colonies are found around the Scottish coastline. Seen high above the sea they are masters of flight, in even the strongest of winds they manoeuvre effortlessly. They are instantly recognisable by their dazzling white plumage with black wing tips and creamy yellow head. In some areas there can be found huge colonies on rocky offshore islands, Bass Rock being one of the more famous. The gannets are probably best known for their spectacular feeding method of diving for fish from up to 30m above the sea's surface. They gather amazing speed with their wings folded back as they dive towards their prey. As they hit the water, split-second timing prevents wings being snapped and a strengthened skull along with air sacks protects the bird's brain from concussion. In the Outer Hebrides a licence is still given for the islanders to hunt these birds, which have been a source of food and oil for remote sea communities for centuries.

Tide & Weather

There are no fast tidal streams on this trip, but the water being forced around Bass Rock does move a bit faster than elsewhere.

Bear in mind that there is nowhere to land on the island so make sure you have planned a rest stop somewhere else.

The channel between Bass Rock and the mainland is used by big ships coming into the inner Firth of Forth. They can appear quite quickly therefore keep an eye open for them.

Additional Information

Parking in North Berwick can be difficult during the holiday season; one option is to drop your kayaks off at the small hidden slipway at the very east end of North Berwick Bay. To find this, go directly toward the harbour and just before it turn left down a narrow road into a courtyard that overlooks the beach and is at the top of the slipway. The parking in here is for the residents, unload your gear and then take your car to the Scottish Seabird car park. You have to pay, but if you go into the Seabird Centre afterwards the parking fee is refunded. An alternative place to launch is into Milsey Bay to the east of the harbour, parking your car on the street adjacent to the beach.

The Scottish Seabird Centre has a website www.seabird.org that provides lots of information about seabirds and it also has web cams, one of which is on Bass Rock.

Tantallon Castle is looked after by Historic Scotland; visit their website www.historic-scotland. gov.uk to find out more about this castle.

St Abb's Head

No. 50 | *Grade B* | *19 or 10km* | *5 or 3 Hours* | *OS Sheet 67* | *Tidal Port Leith*

Start	△ Coldingham Bay (917665)
Finish	◎ Pease Bay (795710) or Coldingham Bay (917665)
HW/LW	HW/LW at St Abbs is about 15 minutes before Leith.
Tidal times	For St Abb's Head: The N going stream starts about 3 hrs and 45 mins after HW Leith. The S going stream starts about 3 hrs and 5 mins before HW Leith.
Tidal rates	The tidal stream is at its fastest off St Abb's and Fast Castle Head. Here the average spring rate can reach 1-2 knots.
Coastguard	Forth, tel:01333 450666, VHF Weather 0730 UT

Introduction

The rock architecture and wildlife of this east coast headland is spectacular enough to impress any sea kayaker. It is a remote and committing section of coastline that has all the ingredients for a great day out. Kayaking amongst the bird life nesting on the cliffs at the St Abb's Head nature reserve is a magical experience.

Description

The picturesque sandy beach of Coldingham provides an ideal place to start a day's paddle around St Abb's Head. Once launched from the sands, the holiday beach environment is left behind for plentiful wildlife and a steep inaccessible coastline. Heading north from Coldingham the quaint village and harbour of St Abbs is soon reached. This is a very popular area for sub-aqua divers, so watch out for their boats and marker buoys. Leaving St Abbs behind, the dominant cliffs of St Abb's Head are all that can be seen, and for the rest of our journey civilisation will seem a long way away. The red volcanic lava cliffs provide plenty of interest with their fantastic shapes and numerous rocky geos and through routes to tempt the inquisitive kayaker. Whilst exploring these cliffs the amount of bird life will gradually increase. During the March – July nesting season there will be thousands of razorbills and guillemots lining the cliffs and flying overhead. Along with these there will be many other seabirds enjoying the perfect nesting platforms that the cliffs of the St Abb's Head nature reserve offers. In these nesting periods it is best to keep a reasonable distance out from the cliffs so as not to disturb the birds from their ledges. Even so with the amount of birds around keep a close eye on crash landing seabirds as they launch from the cliffs!

The lighthouse will soon come into view, which was manned until 1994, and the cliffs in this area are at their most spectacular. Views on up the coastline will soon unfold with the greyer sedimentary rock of Fast Castle Head visible in the distance. Once around St Abb's Head a welcome break in the disused historic harbour of Pettico Wick is recommended. This harbour was built in 1862 to service the lighthouse, before the present day road was built. In 1880 a salmon fishery was also established here and this led to a thriving harbour for many years. These days there are just the ruins of the buildings left, but it provides an idyllically sheltered resting place for the kayaker.

If a shorter day out is preferred this is an ideal place to head back around the cliffs of St Abb's to the beach at Coldingham. If a shuttle has been organised, then continuing on around Fast Castle Head is well recommended.

The coastline on around to Fast Castle Head towers to 160m above the sea. The sedimentary folds of rock and steep grassy hillsides make this an inaccessible part of coastline, with a unique beauty to it. Although not the abundance of nesting birds as St Abb's there are still some large kittiwake colonies. Passing these colonies the bay of Souter is seen, with its old zigzag path still evident that would have been used by fishermen of old. Soon the slender thumb of rock called 'Wheat Stack' will be reached. This has been climbed by rock climbers, as well as some of the other cliffs in this area. The ruined walls of Fast Castle are visible just around the corner, what is left of them balancing precariously on the edge of the cliffs. The rock scenery around Fast Castle Head remains dramatic for a few more kilometres with Bass Rock rising out of the sea in the distance. To stop anywhere along this coastline is awkward, except on very calm days, as the only beaches are made up of large boulders. You may be able to pull ashore at Hirst Rocks for a rest if desired. Here you will see the remains of some ruined fishing houses and cableway to carry the fish caught up the hillside. Leaving here the red sandstone cliffs of Pease Bay, along with Torness Nuclear Power Station will become more and more dominant. After exploring a final cave the sandy beach of Pease Bay will soon be reached, with the caravan park being a contrast to the solitude of the coastline just paddled.

Tide & Weather

This coastline provides limited landing opportunities, with both start and finish beaches having the potential for large surf. With this considered, a day with limited swell and light winds is best.

Having a south-easterly wind and starting from Coldingham when the N going stream begins, 3 hours and 45 minutes after HW Leith, is ideal. As the tides are not too strong along this

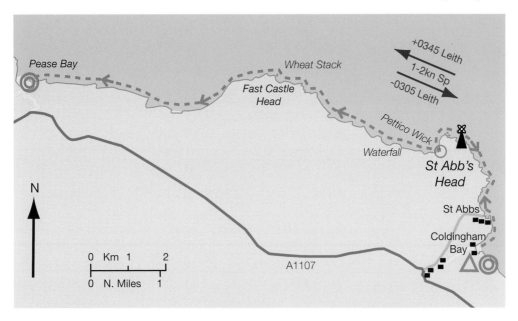

St Abb's Head from rocky landing near Fast Castle Head

coastline it is best to plan to have the wind at your backs for the trip. If this means going against the tide it would give rougher water at the points to be aware of.

If wishing to start and finish at Coldingham then it would be ideal to arrive at Pettico Wick when the S going stream begins, 3 hours and 5 minutes before HW Leith. Leaving Coldingham at about 4 hours and 30 minutes before HW Leith would make this possible. You can paddle against the tide with relative ease on this headland however, so these times are not crucial.

Additional Information

It is possible to launch or land at St Abbs, however it can get very busy with cars and there is a car park charge (£5.00 per day in 2004). If there is a lot of surf at Coldingham or Pease Bay the harbour might be a better alternative. When there is surf there are usually surfers in the water at the beaches, please take care when launching or landing. If the winds are more from the west then starting from Pease Bay may be better. This also saves St Abb's Head until last, which is the highlight of the trip.

Appendix A - Coastguard and Emergency Services

In British waters HM Coastguard coordinates the safe passage of vessels at sea, along with providing emergency rescue cover. There are five HM Coastguard centres that cover all areas along the Scottish coastline. When undertaking a kayaking journey on the sea it is recommended that you inform the relevant Coastguard centre of your intentions, and then let them know when you are off the water. As well as providing emergency rescue cover, the Coastguard can also offer weather, shipping and live firing information. VHF Channel 16 is monitored continually and is to be used if contact with the Coastguard is necessary.

Scotland's HM Coastguard Areas

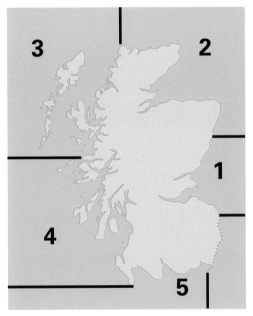

1 Forth Coastguard (Area from English Border to Doonies Point) Tel: 01333 450666. Weather announced on Ch 16: 0130, 0430, 0730, 1030, 1330, 1630, 1930, 2230 UT.

2 Aberdeen Coastguard (Area from Doonies Point to Cape Wrath) Tel: 01224 592334. Weather announced on Ch 16: 0130, 0430, 0730, 1030, 1330, 1630, 1930, 2230 UT.

3 Stornoway Coastguard (Area from Cape Wrath to Adnamurchan Point, including Western Isles) Tel: 01851 702013. Weather announced on Ch 16: 0110, 0410, 0710, 1010, 1310, 1610, 1910, 2210 UT.

4 Clyde Coastguard (Area from Ardnamurchan Point to Mull of Galloway) Tel: 01475 729988. Weather announced on Ch 16: 0210, 0510, 0810, 1110, 1410, 1710, 2010, 2310 UT.

5 Liverpool Coastguard (Area from Mull of Galloway to Queensferry) Tel: 0151 9313341. Weather announced on CH 16: 0130, 0430, 0730, 1030, 1330, 1630, 1930, 2230 UT.

Emergency Telephone Contact

In Great Britain to contact the emergency services by telephone you must dial 999. Having done this you can ask to speak to the Coastguard or Police who coordinate all rescues.

Emergency Mobile Phone Contact

To contact the emergency services on a mobile phone you must dial 112.

Coastguard and Emergency Services

Appendix B - Weather Information

Sources of Weather Forecast:

Television

Detailed Scottish Forecast after local news programmes. BBC at 1855 and 2230 Monday to Friday. Inshore Waters Forecast on Ceefax page 409 and Teletext page 158.

Radio

BBC Radio 4

0048 (LW, MW, FM) – Shipping & Inshore Waters Forecast.
0536 (LW, MW, FM) - Shipping & Inshore Waters Forecast.
1201 (LW only) – Shipping Forecast.
1754 (LW, FM) – Shipping Forecast, Sat/Sun only.

BBC Radio Scotland

1912 (Mon-Fri) – Outdoor Conditions including Inshore Waters Forecast.
0658 & 1858/1958 (Sat/Sun) - Outdoor Conditions including Inshore Waters Forecast.

Inshore Forecast Areas	Shipping Forecast Areas
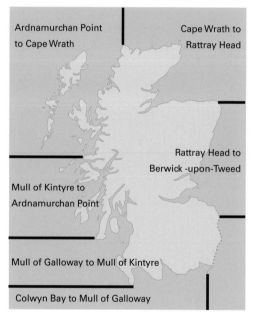	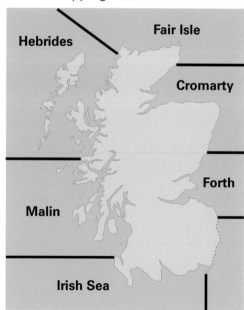

VHF Radio

Every 3 hours the Coastguard broadcasts weather information; this includes the inshore forecasts. The initial call will be made on Channel 16, and this first message will tell you which channel to select to hear the forecast. These forecasts are issued 8 times a day, at 3 hourly intervals and are updated 4 times a day. The time at which each Coastguard transmits the forecast is listed in Appendix A and also in the introduction to each individual trip.

Telephone

Marinecall recorded forecasts for inshore waters. Five areas cover Scotland, dial 09068 5004 + (Area Number).

Inshore and actual weather forecasts can also be obtained by SMS/ texting, on your mobile phone. For further information contact Marinecall at www.marinecall.co.uk or Metmarine at www.metmarine.com .

Fax

Inshore forecasts and synoptic charts are available from Marine Call www.marinecall.co.uk.

Internet

For Inshore Water Forecasts updated at 0500 UT & 1700 UT go to www.metoffice.co.uk.

Marinecall Area Numbers

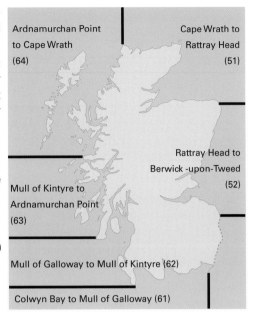

Ardnamurchan Point to Cape Wrath (64)

Cape Wrath to Rattray Head (51)

Rattray Head to Berwick -upon-Tweed (52)

Mull of Kintyre to Ardnamurchan Point (63)

Mull of Galloway to Mull of Kintyre (62)

Colwyn Bay to Mull of Galloway (61)

Weather Averages

Mean Daily Maximum Temperature (C°)

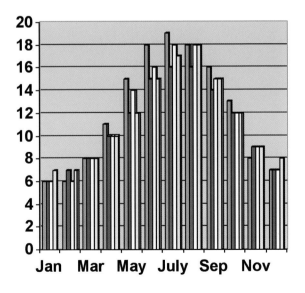

- ■ Glasgow
- ■ Stornoway
- □ Inverness
- □ Fife Ness

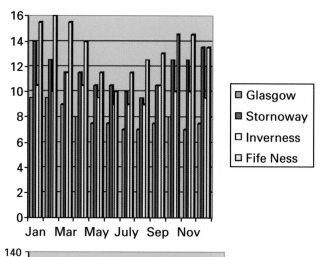

Average Wind Speed
(Knots)

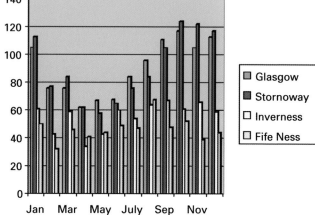

Average Monthly Rainfall
(mm)

Appendix C - Pilots

There are 3 publishers of Pilots in Scotland:

- The Hydrographic Office (Admiralty pilots) www.hydro.gov.uk
- Imray, Laurie, Norie and Wilson www.imray.com
- The Clyde Cruising Club www.clyde.org

Each contains detailed information about tidal streams.

Appendix D - Mean Tidal Ranges

Tidal Port	Mean Spring Range	Mean Neap Range
Dover	6.0m	3.2m
Liverpool	8.4m	4.5m
Greenock	3.1m	1.8m
Oban	3.3m	1.1m
Ullapool	4.5m	1.8m
Aberdeen	3.7m	1.8m
Leith	4.8m	2.4m

Appendix E - Glossary of Gaelic Words

Before the advent of maps and charts the Scottish fishermen navigated the waters by local knowledge. To help them with this they used to descriptively name many of the coastal features, this way they could describe to each other where they went or how to get there. When translating the Gaelic names around the coastline these days you will learn a lot about the area from these very descriptive names. The fishermen only used to fish a relatively small area near to their crofts, and therefore would just name all the features in that area. The next area's fishermen would then name the features in their area likewise. Due to this you will see lots of repetition in the Gaelic names as obviously each area would have its own 'black rock' that it named. Here is a list of some of the more common Gaelic names you will find whilst kayaking the Scottish coastline. A lot of the original mapmakers would have been non-gaelic speaking which is why you'll find variations of spelling. To make matters more complicated, 'local' names, particularly for wildlife can vary from area to area!

Coastal Features

Acairseid	Anchorage	Geò or Geodha	Chasm/Rift
Aiseag	Ferry	Innis	Island or Meadow/Pasture
Ard or Aird	Promontory or Height	Long	Ship
Bàgh	Bay	Mol	Shingly Beach
Bodha	Rock over which waves break	Maol	Promontory
Bogha	Arch	Muir/Mara	Sea/of the sea
Cabhsair	Causeway	Oitir	Sandbank
Cala	Port	Port	Harbour
Camus	Bay/Inlet	Poll	Fishing Bank
Caol or Caolas	Narrows or Kyle/Firth/Strait	Rinn or Roinn	Point or Promontory
Carraig	Rock/Cliff	Rubha, Rubh or Ru	Point/Headland
Ceann	Headland/Point	Sgeir	Skerry/Reef
Cladach	Shore/ Stony Beach	Sròn	Nose/Point
Cleit	Rocky Ridge	Sruth	Current
Coire	Whirlpool	Taobh	Coast
Cuan	Ocean	Traigh	Tidal Beach
Eilean	Island	Uamh	Cave

Land Features

Abhainn	River	Cnap	Hillock
Aill	Steep river bank	Coille	Wood/Forest
Allt	Stream	Creag	Crag/Cliff
Aonach	Moor/Plain/a desert place	Dùn	Fortress/Castle
Bàrr	Top/Summit	Eas or Easan	Waterfall
Bealach	Pass	Fraoch	Heather
Beinn	Mountain	Glac	Hollow
Bidean	Pinnacle	Inbhir	River Mouth
Bruthach	Steep Place/Brae	Linn	Pool
Bun	River Mouth/Source/Root/Base	Meall	Rounded Hill/Mound
Caisteal	Castle	Ord	Steep Hill
Cill or Ceall	Church or Burial Place	Sgùrr	Large Conical Hill
Clach	Stone	Slochd	Hollow
Clais	Ditch	Tigh	House

Common Descriptions for these Features

Ard	High	Geal	White
Bàn	Pale/White	Geàrr	Short
Beag or Bheag	Small	Glas	Pale/Grey
Buidhe	Yellow	Gorm	Green/Blue
Dearg	Red	Liath	Grey/Blue
Dubh	Black/Dark	Mor or Mhor	Big/Large
Domhain	Deep	Naomh	Saint
Donn	Brown	Ruadh	Red/Brown
Fada	Long	Uaine	Green
Garbh	Rough/Thick		

Wild Life

An Leumadair	Dolphin	Iolaire	Eagle
Buthaid	Puffin	Madadh	Wolf/Dog
Caora	Sheep	Muc-mhara	Whale (pig of the sea)
Coinneanach	Rabbit	Puthag	Porpoise
Cù	Dog	Ròn	Seal
Eun-mara	Seabird	Sgarbh	Cormorant
Faoileag	Black Headed Gull	Sùlaire	Gannet
Gille-Brìghde	Oyster Catcher	Trilleachan	Sandpiper
Gobhar	Goat		
Iasg	Fish		

Thanks to Anne Martin for technical comment.

Appendix F - Recommended Reading

The Scottish Islands by Hamish Haswell-Smith ISBN 0 86241 579 9
Collins Encyclopaedia of Scotland edited by John Keay & Julia Keay ISBN 0 00 255082 2
The Yachtsman's Pilots covering Scottish waters produced by Imray, Laurie, Norie & Wilson
The Admiralty Pilots covering Scottish waters, produced by the Hydrographic Office
Field Guide to the Animals of Britain, published by the Readers Digest. ISBN 0 276 36006 0
Field Guide to the Water Life of Britain, published by the Readers Digest. ISBN 0 276 36008 7
The 'Living Landscapes' series published by Scottish Natural Heritage
The 'Naturally Scottish' series, published by Scottish Natural Heritage

Appendix G -Trip Planning Route Card - User's Guide

The trip planning route card is designed to be used in conjunction with the information supplied in each route chapter in the book. In addition to this you will also require a set of relevant tide time tables. If the blank route card is photocopied, all the information for your route to be paddled can be worked out on it. This way it will help you plan your paddle as effectively as possible, and then allow you to have all the information you need on a handy piece of paper. This can be displayed in your map case on your kayak for easy reference.

To help you use the card please refer to the following example and guidelines:

Trip Name and Number	Handa Island, Number 27
Page Number	137
Date of Trip	10th April 2004
Weather Forecast	Sunshine, Clear Visibility, Force 2 wind, Westerly direction, Temperature 12 degrees, Slight sea state.
Coastguard Information	Stornoway Tel: 01851 702013, VHF Weather 0910 UT

- Fill in the name, number and page of your chosen trip for easy future reference.
- When choosing the date of the trip, check in the chapter's 'Tide & Weather' section as to whether it will need specific tides that will dictate the date.
- Obtain a Weather Forecast using information supplied in Appendix B.
- Coastguard Information can be found in the introductory information of each trip and in Appendix A.

Tidal Information

Tidal Port: Ullapool   Mean Sp. Range: 4.5m   Local Port: Scourie
Mean Np. Range: 1.8m

Tidal Port Tide Times (UT)	Height in Metres	Tidal Range in Metres	HW/LW	+1 Hr for BST?	Local Port HW/LW Time Difference	Local Port HW/LW	Sp or Np Tides
0407	1.0		LW	0507	+0010	0517	Between
1013	4.5	3.5	HW	1113	+0010	1123	Between
1632	1.3	3.2	LW	1732	+0010	1742	Between
2244	4.4	3.1	HW	2344	+0010	2354	Between

- Identify Tidal Port from the chapter introductory information.
- Identify Mean Spring and Neap Ranges from tide timetable or see Appendix D. These will help identify Spring or Neap Tides and Estimated Maximum Speed.
- Local Port is also found in the chapter introductory information.
- Obtain the Tidal Port Times and Height in Metres from your tide timetables. Usually four times and heights, but occasionally three.
- To work out the Tidal Range in Metres subtract the LW heights from the HW heights.
- Is 1 Hr added for BST? Add an hour to your Tidal Port Times if you are in British Summer Time.
- The Local Port HW/LW Time Difference can be found in the chapter introductory information.
- To work out Spring or Neap Tides compare your Tidal Range in Metres to the Mean Sp and Np Ranges.

Tidal Stream Times

Location	Direction of Tidal Stream	Tidal Stream Time Diff.	Tidal Port HW (BST?)	Tidal Stream Start Time	Tidal Rate	Est. Max Speed
W Coast Handa	SW	+0430	2245	0315	3 knots	2.25 knots
	NE	-0145	1113	0928	3 knots	2.25 knots
	SW	+0430	1113	1543	3 knots	2.25 knots

Location	Direction of Tidal Stream	Tidal Stream Time Diff.	Tidal Port HW (BST?)	Tidal Stream Start Time	Tidal Rate	Est. Max Speed
	NE	-0145	2344	2159	3 knots	2.25 knots
Sound of Handa	SW	+0210	2245	0055	3 knots	2.25 knots
	NE	- 0415	1113	0658	3 knots	2.25 knots
	SW	+ 0210	1113	1323	3 knots	2.25 knots
	NE	- 0415	2344	1929	3 knots	2.25 knots

- Use the Location as indicated in the chapter introductory and tidal information.
- For the Direction of Tidal Stream there are generally four periods of tidal stream movement in a 24 hour period. You want the direction that Tidal Stream Start Time is soonest after 0000 hours in the first box.
- The Tidal Stream Time Difference is found in the chapter introductory and tidal information.
- The Tidal Port HW can be found in the previously filled out information. Remember to note the BST time if appropriate.
- The Tidal Stream Start Time is worked out by subtracting/adding the Tidal Stream Difference from/to the Tidal Port HW time.
- The Tidal Rate is the average spring speed for the tidal stream, this is found in the chapter introductory and tidal information.
- To Estimate Maximum Speed refer to previous information to see whether it is Spring, Neap or in between tides.
- If it is Springs use the speed given in the chapters introductory and tidal information.
- On Neap Tides half this spring rate.
- When in between springs and neaps use the average of the spring and neap speeds.
- Note that speeds given are average spring rates. If paddling on a spring tide look to see if your Tidal Range in Metres is bigger or smaller than the Mean Sp Range. If it is bigger the speeds will be faster than average spring rates given.

Route Plan

	Name	Notes	ETA	ETD
Start Place	Scourie			1300
1st Location	Port a Eilean	First stopping place, beach.	1345	1430
2nd Location	Great Stack	Need to be here as tide starts S.W.	1543	1550
3rd Location	Tarbet	Second stopping place, tearoom.	1620	1700
4th Location				
5th Location				
Finish Place	Scourie			1800

- When choosing Locations for the Route Plan use places that have tidal importance and where you may want to stop.
- When working out ETD (Estimated Time of Departure) or ETA (Estimated Time of Arrival) enter key times which need to be met for the best use of tidal stream first, as recommended in Tide & Weather (Great Stack in the example above). Work out other times around these.
- To work out the times an average paddling speed of 6km/h or 3 knots can be used. This can be adjusted to suit your needs, or time added for coastal exploration if desired.

Trip Planning Route Card

Trip Name and Number	
Page Number	
Date of Trip	
Weather Forecast	
Coastguard Information	

Tidal Information

Tidal Port: Mean Sp Range: Local Port:

Mean Np Range:

Tidal Port TideTimes (UT)	Height in Metres	Tidal Range in Metres	HW/LW	+1 Hr for BST?	Local Port HW/LWTime Difference	Local Port HW/LW	Sp or Np Tides

Tidal Stream Times

Location	Direction of Tidal Stream	Tidal Stream Time Diff.	Tidal Port HW (BST?)	Tidal Stream Start Time	Tidal Rate	Est. Max Speed

Location	Direction of Tidal Stream	Tidal Stream Time Diff.	Tidal Port HW (BST?)	Tidal Stream Start Time	Tidal Rate	Est. Max Speed

Location	Direction of Tidal Stream	Tidal Stream Time Diff.	Tidal Port HW (BST?)	Tidal Stream Start Time	Tidal Rate	Est. Max Speed

Route Plan

	Name	Notes	ETA	ETD
Start Place				
1st Location				
2nd Location				
3rd Location				
4th Location				
5th Location				
Finish Place				

Index

Index

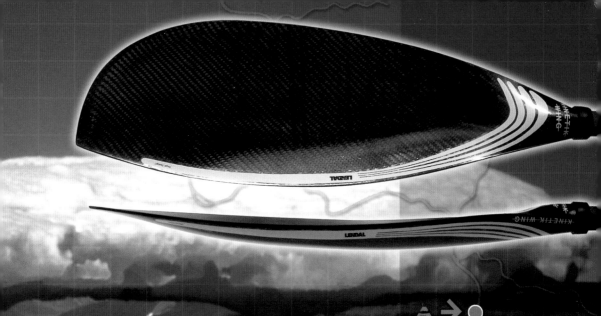

KNOYDART

OPEN WATER TOURING SPECIALISTS

sea kayaks
- VALLEY
- NIMBUS
- EPIC
- SKIM

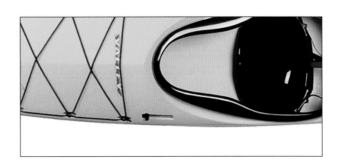

folding boats
- FEATHERCRAFT
- KLEPPER
- PAKBOAT

paddles
- EPIC
- NIMBUS
- LENDAL

clothing
- KOKATAT

saling rigs
- BALOGH
- FEATHERCRAFT
- KLEPPER

accessories
- PDF'S
- SPRAYDECKS
- DRY BAGS
- DECK BAGS
- SAFETY EQUIPMENT
- CAMPING EQUIPMENT
- TRANSPORTING BOATS
- BOOKS

Hartness Road, Gillwilly Industrial Estate, Penrith, Cumbria, CA11 9BD

01768 840 055   www.knoydart.co.uk   df@knoydart.co.uk